Sell Our Australian Farm?
You've Got to be Kidding!

Sell Our Australian Farm?
You've Got to be Kidding!

A Moore Family Odyssey, Book Three
Connie Moore

Belleville, Ontario, Canada

Sell Our Australian Farm? You've Got to be Kidding!

Copyright © 2004, Connie Moore

All Rights Reserved. No part of this publication may be reproduced, stored in a retrieval system or transmitted in any form or by any means—electronic, mechanical, photocopy, recording or any other—except for brief quotations in printed reviews, without the prior permission of the author.

Library and Archives Canada Cataloguing in Publication

Moore, Connie, 1930-
    Sell our Australian farm? You've got to be kidding! / Connie Moore.

(A Moore family odyssey ; Bk. 3)
ISBN 1-55306-860-2

    1. Moore, Connie, 1930- 2. Farm life--Australia. 3. Farmers' spouses--Australia--Biography. I. Title. II. Series: Moore, Connie, 1930- . Moore family odyssey ;Bk. 3

DU117.2.M66A3 2004   630'.92   C2004-906396-0

**For more information or
to order additional copies, please contact:**

Connie Moore
9701 East Hwy. 25, #176
Belleview, FL 34420 USA
Phone/Fax: (352) 347-5492

Epic Books is an imprint of *Essence Publishing,* a Christian Book Publisher dedicated to furthering the work of Christ through the written word. For more information, contact:

20 Hanna Court, Belleville, Ontario, Canada K8P 5J2
Phone: 1-800-238-6376 • Fax: (613) 962-3055
E-mail: publishing@essencegroup.com
Internet: www.essencegroup.com

Table of Contents

Acknowledgements 7
Meet the Family 9
Foreword 11
Preface 13
Prologue 15

1. Day by Day 17
2. The Christmas Boat 27
3. The Ping-Pong Club 37
4. Rainy Days 45
5. The Power Cometh 55
6. The Pot Simmers 63
7. Catching Up 73
8. Moving Dirt 79
9. Changes 87
10. A Boat to Float 97
11. The Essay 107
12. Fun and Games 113
13. Will It Ever End? 121
14. Aunt Jac 131

15. Will She or Won't She? 139
16. Things to Make 147
17. A Son Is Grown 155
18. A New Era 161
19. God Still Does Miracles 171
20. Growing Pains 179
21. Surprises 185

Acknowledgements

This book is dedicated to my husband Bill and our children: Rusty, Mickey, Skippy, Tia, Pam, Jackie and Topper. Without them there would be no story. Together we lived it and together we wrote it. Our lives entwined have been captured on these pages. We wish you pleasure in getting to know us.

*Boys: Left to Right, Topper, Mickey, Skippy, Rusty.
Girls: Left to Right, Pam, Jackie, Tia.*

Meet the Family

Rusty, a sixteen-year-old red head, resembles his dad. Mature for his age, he is an excellent student and a great help on the farm. His interests are fishing, boats and girls, in that order. Fortunately, in Australia, it's okay to like fishing more than girls. Girls will come later. Adventure comes first.

Mickey, a blond fourteen-year-old, is a teenager who has discovered "The Great Truth": his parents are hopelessly old fashioned! An enterprising boy with a sense of humor, he continues his interest in architecture with landscape gardening as an added feature.

Skippy, a twelve-year-old brunet, is at the top of his class. He has always been his father's boy and works well with him when the other boys are busy. He enjoys the challenge of daring deeds and reacts quickly in an emergency.

Tia is a typical blond nine-year-old. She excels at school and loves to do creative handiwork. She's a wonderful big sister to Pam and Jackie and a self-appointed "second mom" to Topper. With her active imagination, she entertains all three with story-telling and games.

Pam, a blond, petite six-year-old, is usually found with a pencil in her hand. Curious about everything, she devours school in great gulps. Taking advantage of the two-room school system, she memorizes the second- and third-grade poems as well as those of her first grade.

Jackie is a four-year-old strawberry blond with a smattering of freckles. Best described as precocious, she never meets a stranger. She's lost with Pam away at school and is counting the days until she can join her. Topper helps fill the void.

Topper, at the age of two, is a sturdy little mechanized blond. He seldom moves without turning on his motor. His "brrrmmm, brrmmm" can be heard all over the house. I say, "Come here, Topper, I want to tuck in your shirt." He shifts himself into reverse gear to back up; sometimes it requires a three-point maneuver—he does know the difference. For such a little fellow, he is surprisingly neat and tidy and always ready to lend a helping hand.

Foreword

Women of Fiddler's Green

"Just in case you didn't know it, calm weather and smooth seas are the result of the sweet songs of the women of Fiddler's Green, who sing to keep the waves in unison. Whenever they stop singing, the waves get restless and bad weather ensues."

The *"Women of Fiddler's Green"* is an excerpt from the book *Traditions of the Navy* by Cedric W. Windas. Davy Jones' Locker is a mythical place deep in the ocean where sailors go. Fiddler's Green is where good sailors go. Dad was a good sailor who found a place of quiet and peace, not in the deep but on Russell Island. Mom named our place "Fiddler's Green."

That must be why Mom sang a lot—to keep things on an even keel. Mom sang through the good and the bad, soothing feelings and bringing life back into balance. What a beautiful way to look at the small kingdom we built on Russell Island. Adversity gave us a reason to be strong as a family and to be innovative in many ways. One of these was to find a strong and meaningful name for our island farm. Mom did it again.

— Michael James Moore (Mickey)

Preface

In this book I have endeavored to render the truth as accurately as possible. Even though this is my story, it includes many other people who played major or minor roles. In some situations names have been changed.

Dialogue and events are reported to the best of my recollection. Although circumstances are accurate, I cannot be certain every quote is entirely accurate or word for word. In many cases my interpretation of events will perhaps differ from another's memory.

Much time has passed since many of these events occurred. This book is intended to preserve a time in the history of a specific family. If you see the events portrayed differently than your memory of them, it doesn't mean that either of us is wrong. We all have uniquely different personalities and perspectives.

—Connie Moore

Russell Island

The largest of the R.K.L.M. group, Russell Island is a subtropical haven in Tranquil Moreton Bay
  ✳ Fiddler's Green

Prologue

Book one of a four-book series, *Move to Australia? You've Got to be Kidding!* is a heartwarming tale that is both captivating and informative. It begins in the early 1960s with the idea of emigrating to Australia. In America, children had rooms full of toys but lacked a sense of responsibility. Captivated by television, they were missing the challenge of outside play. Connie and Bill wanted more traditional values for their family. When Bill retires from the U.S. Navy, the "idea" becomes reality.

With their six children, they sail to the land "down under." At Sydney they buy a mini van and head to Western Australia, three thousand miles away. Full of adventure, the trip takes them across the desolate, unpaved Nullabor Plain. There are no hotels, motels or restaurants, only a few small towns in which to stock up on gas and groceries. Traveling back east, they settle in Brisbane, Queensland—but not for long. Bill discovers the perfect place to raise children. "It's a farm on an island in Redland Bay," he tells Connie, "we can all be farmers."

Book two of the series, *Me? An Australian Farmer? You've got to be kidding!* covers the comedy and pathos of learning to farm in a strange, hemispherically upside-down country. The family copes with a phone service that only operates from 8 A.M to 8 P.M., a pony that refuses to stay at home and a farm they nickname "Broken-Downsville."

In this different world, chickens are "chooks." Bananas are "trashed." Shoppers carry their own "tucker" bags. Christmas is celebrated during the heat of summer and the new school year starts in January.

A delightful event in this topsy-turvy story is the birth of a baby boy. This new "littlie" sleeps in a bureau drawer. The household shipment is late. When six overseas crates arrive from the States, chaos reigns. Each room-sized crate holds treasures they have not seen for a year. Weeks of opening ceiling-high piles of boxes proves to be more exciting than Christmas and all the birthdays lumped together.

As farmers-in-training the family becomes less of a "comedy act." They make friends with the islanders and develop new skills. The children excel at school. Broken-Downsville becomes Fiddler's Green, a place of peace and rest. The crops are growing well. The future looks bright.

But clouds are gathering on the horizon. "Winds of change" begin to blow across the island. They intensify with the arrival of a new neighbor. One who hates Americans. More change is yet to come.

Chapter One

Day by Day

I sat in the gazebo at Fiddler's Green making plans for the upcoming holidays. Mentally, I tried to locate our box of Halloween costumes. We had toted that box around the world and stowed it away in many different houses. But where did I put it when we unpacked our shipment from the States? Oh, yes! I remember now. It's up on the shelf in the boy's closet. Mystery solved. I smiled as visions of children and costumes tumbled through my mind. They began to emerge in verse:

There is a box upon the shelf
of fairies, witches and little elves.
Angel wings when Pam was two,
A bunny play for Mickey to do.

A pirate for Rusty on Halloween,
Skip, a tiger and Tia, a queen.

Jackie, a bunny with floppy ears,
Topper the cowboy without any fears.

Special days we shared together
Each one built upon another.
Seven souls entwined with mine
Fleeting past, from out of time.

Laughter, tears and fruitful days,
Paths to guide in seven ways.
As time goes by I pray each day
That God will bless and lead the way.

A feeling of nostalgia washed over me. *Children grow up too fast, I sighed. Just when I think I know what I'm doing, they take another leap forward.*

As if on cue, Bill climbed up into the gazebo to join me. "What's the matter?" he asked.

"I was just thinking about life. What are you up to?"

"I'm taking a break and this is the most comfortable place to do it."

"Jolly good! Who would have thought part of our little Vanguard would be turned into a gazebo? I don't understand how you and the boys managed to lift it up onto old Rackety Boom."

"Rackety Boom" was a 1929 pickup truck that came with the farm. It got its nickname from one of the children's books. In the story, Rackety Boom was a nice old truck. It didn't go very far or very fast. Sometimes, it just stood still—on the top of a hill...much like our truck. Shortly after we moved to the farm old Rackety Boom wouldn't go at all.

Eventually we became owners of a small European sedan. Bill decided to make the 1950s Vanguard into a utility truck by removing the seats and roof from the frame. After Mickey used a chisel to cut across the roof just behind the windshield, they looked for a place to put the section they were removing.

Rackety Boom was parked nearby and the truck bed was empty. Between them, Bill and the boys hoisted the whole section up onto the truck. A cozy perch, sheltered from the sun and the rain. We dubbed it "the gazebo" and often used it as a quick getaway spot.

"It was a big job," Bill admitted. "But at least we're getting some use out of this old truck." He peered over my shoulder. "What are you writing?"

"A poem. Want to hear it?"

"Sure." He settled back against the cushions as I read the poem. When I finished, we were quiet for a while. Finally, he spoke. "They've grown some since then, haven't they?"

"I know. Our little pirate is now sixteen years old. It's hard to believe that box of costumes has been around since Japan."

"That's a lot of years," Bill mused. "Skippy, the tiger. Did you ever imagine he would be a high-jump champion at school?"

"No, but when he runs, he floats on the wind, like poetry in motion. Sort of like a tiger, I guess."

Bill grinned. "I can't picture our fourteen-year-old doing a bunny play, either."

I sighed. "Mickey's just flexing his muscles of teenage independence. But you'll have to admit, Tia is still a queen. She knows what she wants and goes after it."

"Too right, but is Pam still an angel?"

"If angels organize everyone and know how much they can get away with, I suppose so."

"Who's an angel?" Mickey asked, looking in the window.

"You are," I smiled. "Hey! I just remembered where I put the costumes."

"Fair dinkum?" he grinned. "We might need them for Halloween." He looked at his dad. "I finished hoeing the rows. Can Topper and I drive the Ladybug down to the jetty to get Rusty?" The "Ladybug" was what we called the small truck made from the Vanguard frame. It was perfect for harvesting crops and running errands. Bill nodded okay. Mickey scooped up Topper. "We can go," he said, tickling his tummy.

I looked down at my watch. "Goodness, is it that late! I'd better get dinner ready." Quickly, I gathered my things together. Bill climbed out and lifted me down from the gazebo.

I almost landed on Jackie who had come to plead her case. "Mom, I'm hungry," she wailed, "when's dinner?"

Taking her by the hand, I comforted her. "We're going to get it ready right now." As we climbed the steps, I outlined the game plan. "Mickey and Topper have gone to get Rusty. They'll be back soon. You and Tia set the table. Pam and I will get the food ready." As soon as we entered the door, she ran down the hall shouting, "Tia! Pam! Mom wants you! It's dinnertime."

Rusty's school day starts with a mile walk to the jetty, followed by a forty-five minute school boat trip to pick up students from the other islands. And, finally, a twenty-minute bus ride from Redland Bay to Cleveland High School. It's a long day. By the time he gets home to Fiddler's Green, dinner is the most important thing on his mind.

"Hi, Mom, smells wonderful," he sniffed, carrying Topper through the door.

"It's your favorite meat loaf," I greeted him.

"The table is set for dinner," Tia announced, peering around the corner.

"Good job, go tell Dad and the others it's dinnertime."

As each day winds down, we are blessed by being able to eat together as a family. Conversation flows around the table. Everyone has something to offer. This evening, Rusty was first to share his news. "I talked to Mrs. Robinson on the boat today."

"Oh, how is Hypatia and what did she have to say?"

"Her mother is sick and she's going back to Jersey to stay with her for a while."

"Oh dear. We'll certainly miss her."

"Where's Jersey?" Pam asked.

When we all looked blank, Dad enlightened us. "Jersey is one of the Channel Islands off the coast of France. By the way," he looked at me, "Curtis Routledge has a job on Stradbroke Island with a sand mining company. Today he told me they might go over there to live."

"Oh, my goodness," I moaned, "first the Grahams moved to a new school post, then Hypatia and now the Routledges. The island really is changing."

"Yes," Mickey said, "it started changing when the Grahams left. They were our best friends and helped us get used to island living."

Tia agreed, "Mrs. Graham was the nicest teacher I ever had."

Pam piped up, "Michael Graham was my best friend."

"Let's send them a card!" Jackie said, always ready with a comforting thought. "We can make one after dinner."

It was time to change the subject. "Speaking of making things…what are we going to do for Halloween?"

"Let's hire the hall and have a party," Rusty suggested. "We can invite all the kids from the other islands. I'll do my magic tricks for entertainment."

"That's a great idea. The kids would like that." I looked at Mickey. "I saw you having fun with the kids at the Sunday school picnic. Would you do some of those games and folk dances for the party?"

"I guess," he ventured.

"It might be fun to put on a little play," I suggested. "Skippy, would you check our Pack-O-Fun books for a Halloween skit?"

"What can we do?" the girls asked, almost in unison.

"You can help me with the invitations."

The project was on! The next day, I cut Casper the Ghost shapes from construction paper and drew a smiling face on each one.

"I like happy ghosts," Pam approved, looking over my shoulder.

On the outside I wrote, "An invitation from the Moores." I typed a little verse for the inside.

"What does it say?" Jackie asked, gluing the verse in place.

"It says," I read:

"Halloween is here again!
We're having a party too.
So put on your costume
And come to the hall.
We'll be waiting for you."

"I hope we won't have to wait too long for them to get there," Jackie said, giggling at her own joke.

When the invitations were finished, Tia pleaded, "Can we deliver them now?"

"Yes, but don't stay at anyone's house. It's almost dinner time." They skipped down the steps, chattering about where they would go first.

When I passed Skippy's room, he was sitting on the floor surrounded by Pack-O-Fun books. "Did you find a skit?" I asked.

"Yes, ma'am," he said proudly, passing me one of the books.

I sat down to read. The play was about two boys who entered an empty house on Halloween. With ghostly moans and clanking chains, they planned to scare anyone who passed by. Surprisingly, two other boys had the same idea. Their antics fooled all of them into thinking that ghosts were really haunting the house. The play ends when the frightened boys, trying to get away from the "real" ghosts, bump into each other.

"Wonderful," I applauded. It was a good skit that, thankfully, required very few props.

On party day, the girls helped bake cookies and make sandwiches. Bill and the boys went down to decorate the hall. When everything was ready, Bill hooked the trailer up to the tractor. We loaded it with food, games and people and headed for the hall.

Twenty children arrived to join in the fun. We started the evening with apple bobbing, egg races and relays. After things quieted down, Rusty set up a table to begin his magic act. All his hours of practice paid off. He astounded everybody by making things vanish and reappear in unexpected places. When the kids tried to detect his secrets, he nonchalantly shrugged his shoulders. "It's just magic," he smiled, with a straight face and mysterious air.

When it was time for Mickey to entertain, he was suddenly very quiet. I sat down beside him. "What's the matter?" I asked with concern.

He shrugged. "Nothin'."

"Aren't you going to do the games and folk dances?"

"They've already played games. I just want to do the skit."

Disappointed, I rounded up the cast and introduced the skit. Joining Bill on a bench, I muttered, "How do you figure teens? I hope Mickey does well in the skit."

He did. Everyone roared when the "ghosts" got spooked backing into each other. Without realizing they had bumped into friends, they all ran in different directions screaming loudly. End of play. The kids went wild. After they settled down, we served refreshments and gave out prizes.

As the children began to leave, one of the parents commented, "This has been a great evening. It's not surprising that everyone wonders what you people will do next." I took that as a compliment. Little did I realize that our "farmers-in-training" Pig Caper would be even more entertaining.

The Pig Caper started out as a pronouncement at dinner when Dad said, "I just bought a couple of little piglets from Mr. Padden. We have a lot of sweet potatoes that are too small for market. I'd like to turn them into an advantage for us. We can use them to feed the pigs."

Mickey frowned darkly. Still struggling with the idea that adults were really dumb, "Here we go again," he muttered. He was right. Within a week, the pigs had gotten out of the pen and were back at Mr. Padden's farm.

After a couple of repeat performances, Bill constructed a pen that strongly resembled the security of a bank vault. "That should do it," he declared, putting the pigs back in for the third time. It worked. The pigs stayed home.

One day, making our rounds of the farm, we walked up the hill to check on the pigs. "Hon," I asked, leaning over the fence, "how long does it take for pigs to get fat? There are still a lot of potatoes to eat but the pigs aren't growing any bigger."

Bill frowned. "Something's crook."

"What do you mean, 'crook'?"

"That's Australian for 'not good,'" he sighed, feeling that I should have known that by now. He turned back to the pigs. "This is the first time I've been up here for a while. I'm sure the boys have been feeding them table scraps and plenty of potatoes but they're still too small. I'll ask Mr. Padden. He might be able to tell me what's wrong."

I had tea and cookies ready when Bill came back from Mr. Padden's. Sitting down at the table, he shook his head. "Pig raising is more complicated than I thought."

"Fair dinkum?" I asked.

"Too right! This is the problem. They're only eating table scraps because they aren't old enough to chew the sweet potatoes. Mr. Padden says their food has to be chopped and cooked until they get bigger."

"Wow, why didn't he tell you that sooner? That's a big job."

"Too right! I knew it would be difficult for us to do, so I struck a bargain. He'll take our pigs back and I'll supply enough sweet potatoes to feed all the pigs, his and ours, until they're grown. He already has equipment set up to do the job. Our extra sweet potatoes will be a big help for him."

"My goodness," I said, amazed. "I thought pigs would eat anything."

Bill shrugged his shoulders. "So did I. I guess we still have a lot to learn about being farmers."

"Don't feel bad," I sympathized, "kid-raising is more interesting, anyway. Want another cookie?"

Chapter Two

The Christmas Boat

"Let's go for a walk," Bill suggested, after Topper and the girls had been tucked in for the night. Evening walks were our special time: an opportunity to carry on adult conversation without juvenile questions and comments. I looked around. The boys had finished the dishes and were busy with their homework. Everything was in order. "Righto, I'm ready!"

We stepped out into the dark starry night and headed toward the road. Feeling the tensions of the day dissolve, I inhaled deep breaths of fresh clean air. We were so blessed to be able to walk in the cool of the evening. No traffic, no smog, no—oops. I had forgotten the round, volcanic pebbles just under the red dirt.

"Watch your step," Bill said, taking my arm. "Those rocks are slippery!"

"Ah, yes, but it's so good to be out here. Jackie and Pam have been after me all day to help them with Christmas gifts they're making. With all the year-end festivities next month, who has time for farming? Maybe it's a just as well the tractor isn't working."

"Too right," Bill declared. "We can't get anything done on the farm until the new water pump arrives for the tractor. But there are plenty other things that need attention. It's been almost two years since we brought our boat in on a king tide [that's Australian for "spring tide"] and beached it at Ron and Jack's. I told the boys yesterday, if we work together, we could have it running by Christmas."

"Wonderful, what do we have to do?"

"A lot. For starters, it needs a new inboard motor, several planks will have to be replaced and there are holes to patch."

"Well, I don't know about those things, but I do know it needs a lot of paint. I can do that. When do we start the project?"

"Well, since there is no moon tonight, we can expect the new moon to bring in a high tide in a couple of days. When that happens, we'll prop the boat upright and begin working."

Everyone was excited about the idea of resurrecting the *Seagull*. "Let's make it a picnic," Tia suggested.

"Good idea. This project can be a Sunday afternoon picnic event until the boat is done."

On the next king tide, Bill and the boys tipped the boat upright and secured it with posts. On the following Sunday, we began our picnic working bees. Bill replaced the motor, put in a new bilge pump and repaired rotted planks. The rest of his "crew" patched holes while the littlies played on the beach.

The boat became a neighborhood project when Jack Saunders dropped by to look things over. He admired what we had done so far but reckoned, "It would be a good idea to fiberglass the bottom after you get it painted."

"Fair dinkum?" Bill asked. "How do I do that?"

"It's not difficult," Jack explained. "You paint on a coat of rosin, put on the fiberglass cloth and paint another coat to seal it. When you're ready, I'll come down and we'll give it a go."

Bill made a special trip to the mainland to pick up materials for the job. At home, he explained what had to be done. "It's going to be a messy job. We'll need to keep a fire going to heat the rosin. For obvious reasons, you and the littlies can have the afternoon off. I'll just take the boys as helpers."

The following week Curtis, Ron and Jack arrived at the beach for a working bee. The boys found wood to keep the fire burning and stood by to help as offsiders. At the end of the day, Jack appraised the work. He announced with satisfaction, "Give it a while to set and it will keep you dry and snug."

On the next king tide, Bill and the boys removed the props and let the boat settle into the water. It passed the test! Happily there were no leaks. Bill used the rowboat to anchor it just off the beach in the channel.

Jack, the expert carpenter, made another suggestion. "Your rowboat is too big. You need a little dinghy to tow behind the boat. It will be handy when you have to anchor off shore. If you have the lumber sent over, I'll show you how to make one."

While Bill and Jack worked on the eight-foot dinghy, Mickey and I talked about painting the deck and cabin. "Let's row out to see what needs to be done," Mickey suggested.

"Jolly good! Then we'll know what to bring with us when we start the job." We rowed out in the dinghy and climbed aboard to survey the twelve-foot cabin.

"Goodness," I exclaimed, looking things over, "this is going to take days of scrubbing, scraping, patching, pounding and painting." The next Sunday, we rowed out with cleaning supplies, tools, putty and sandpaper to begin—what we hoped—would be a miracle transformation.

"Wouldn't it be great to have it done by Christmas?" Mickey fancied, scrubbing the bunk areas.

"Impossible," I grunted, sandpapering a stubborn area of old paint.

"Since it's summer vacation and Dad doesn't need me, we could come down every afternoon," Mickey persisted.

"What about Topper?"

"Bring him with us."

"You're kidding. How long do you think a two-and-a-half-year-old would last in a little area like this? And what about all the paint and stuff?"

"He'll be all right. I'll watch him. Please..." he coaxed.

There was still a lot of work to do and Christmas was getting close. Packing up for the day, I relented, "We'll give it a jolly try. It'll be a good change for Topper and a nice break for Tia."

The next day we loaded wood for repairs, paint supplies and Topper into the dinghy. Once on the boat, he found plenty to do. He especially liked the challenge of walking on the narrow ledge past the cabin to the bow and back again. "Be sure to hang on tight," I cautioned him.

"I will," he promised, beaming with confidence.

"You keep an eye on him, Mickey. I'll start painting inside." I was crawling around in the cabin, balancing a paint can in one hand and brush in the other, when I heard a big splash. I popped my head out the cabin window. Topper was in the water, paddling wildly trying to keep afloat. Amazed, I saw Mickey calmly lower one leg into the water as a lifeline. Topper grabbed his foot and hung on. Mickey hoisted him up onto the deck, safe and sound.

Slowly, my lungs began to fill with air. My heart began to beat again. My mind cautioned me—stay positive. Picking up Topper, I cuddled him in my lap. "You're going to be a great swimmer!" I praised him. Looking up, I shot Mickey a frown that said, "See, I told you so."

"I knew he was okay," Mickey said with a grin. I had to admit—he was right.

Despite the tense moments and hard work, it was pleasant being out in the bay in a gently rocking boat. Several times, when it was quiet, I heard someone heave a great sigh. Who could it be? I searched the water for a swimmer. I scanned the shore. There was no one in sight. How odd, I puzzled. It was a mystery.

One day I happened to look up just as the football-sized head of a giant turtle broke water to breathe. "Oh my goodness, Mickey, did you see that!" I called. "A giant sea turtle! That's where those sighs have been coming from!"

"It must weigh close to 300 pounds!" Mickey exclaimed. "Do we have a story to tell at dinner tonight! The mystery has been solved."

The family was impressed with the turtle story, but really wanted to know when the boat would be ready. Soon, we assured them.

When the painting was finished, I covered new cushions for the bunks and made matching curtains for the windows. Bill rowed out with us to help with the finishing touches. With everything in place, we admired our handiwork.

"Looks great," Bill said, "want to take a test run?"

"Can we go to Kerr's on Macleay Island?" Mickey asked. "That would be a nice practice trip."

Bill started the motor and cruised out into the bay. We were underway! Fifteen minutes later, we anchored offshore and rowed in to the beach on Macleay. The Kerrs were surprised to see us and wondered how we had gotten to the island.

"We came in the *Seagull*," Mickey told them.

"The *Seagull*?"

"Yes, that's the name of our boat." Proudly, he explained that our twenty-foot launch was finally afloat.

After a short visit and feeling very "islandish," we headed back to the *Seagull*. "How exciting to have our own means of transportation," I boasted as we walked down to the beach.

By the time we reached the jetty, the tide had changed. It was going out—and so was our boat! I looked on in horror. Always quick to act, Bill jumped into the dinghy, rowed out to the drifting *Seagull* and towed it back. Lesson number one: there is a trick to anchoring boats, depending on whether the ocean bottom is sand or rocks and what kind of anchor you're using. "It may take a while but we'll get the hang of it," Bill said, confidently.

I nodded, but I didn't comment. I had an uneasy feeling that water transportation was not going to be my favorite means of travel. Of course, I was outnumbered; everyone else was thrilled with the boat.

"Can we go to Brown's pool for Christmas?" Jackie cooed, climbing onto her daddy's lap after dinner.

"That would be fun," Tia called from the kitchen, where she was decorating Christmas "bickies" (Aussie nickname for cookies). Down under, cookies are biscuits and biscuits are scones. While we worked on the boat, Tia had been a wonderful help with Topper and loved making covered dishes and biscuits to take to Christmas parties.

The words, "Brown's pool" had a magical ring. Suddenly, everyone clustered around Dad, waiting for an answer. "That's why we worked so hard," Mickey prodded.

"What do you think?" Bill asked, glancing at me. His face was serious but I could see a chuckle in his eye.

Catching the spirit, I teased, "What about Christmas dinner? It takes all afternoon to cook a duck."

"Wouldn't it be nice," Rusty asked quietly, "to christen the *Seagull* on Christmas Day?"

"Well," I paused, assured of everyone's attention. "We could put the duck in the oven and let it cook while we're gone." That did it! Mom had saved the day.

Christmas morning we hurriedly opened our gifts with our minds on the planned cruise. One very special gift was a beautiful handmade guitar. Jack had crafted three of them, one for himself, one for Ron and one for me. I had never seen anyone make a guitar before. I couldn't imagine being able to do that. Jack was an excellent woodworker. I felt special and honored.

After our Christmas breakfast of bacon, eggs and the traditional Australian hot cross buns, I prepared two ducks for the oven. Bill stoked up the stove and we headed for the boat.

While we waited at the jetty for Dad to bring in the boat, Mickey reminded me, "We have to christen the boat before we can go anywhere,"

"Yes, where's the champagne bottle?" Rusty asked.

"Sorry," I said, "we'll have to settle for a little water and a lot of imagination."

The tide was low so we climbed down to the cement platform while Bill moored the boat. Everyone gathered around as Dad began the ceremony. He poured water from a wine bottle over the bow while he solemnly intoned, "I christen you... the *Seagull*." We all clapped and cheered.

"Now," he said, lifting Topper and the girls aboard, "let's see how this *Seagull* can fly." The weather was ideal for our maiden voyage. The little ones had life jackets on and the tide was almost low enough to walk home—if we had to. I took a deep breath and realized it would be all right to relax.

We sailed past Karragarra and around to the northern tip of Russell Island to Brown's place. It was a stop-off point for sailboats traveling down to the Gold Coast from Brisbane. There were picnic tables, cabins for overnight guests and a salt water swimming pool.

Mr. Brown came out to greet us. "Today," he said, with a grin, "you have the pool all to yourselves. There are no boaters here and our three boys are out fishing."

"This is our second Christmas here," Skippy informed him. "Last year we came in our Christmas car. This year we came in our Christmas boat."

"She's a real beaut," Mr. Brown said admiring the shiny paint job. "Looks like a brand new boat to me." He waved his hand at the pool. "It's all yours, enjoy!"

"Jolly good," Tia yelled, jumping into the cool water. The rest followed her lead.

After a pleasant afternoon of "Mom, look at me!" and "Dad, watch this!" it was time to go. We packed up and headed the *Seagull* toward home.

When we arrived, the ducks were just right for a candle-lit Christmas feast with all the trimmings. Especially the pumpkin and mincemeat pies. Mincemeat, my favorite Christmas pie, is not an Australian custom. Luckily, on a trip to Brisbane, we had found a jar of mincemeat imported from Canada.

"This is a Christmas to remember," Bill toasted. "Let's hope 1967 will be a bonus year for the Moores. The fields are full of sweet potatoes. The price is good. The drought has broken."

Chapter Three

The Ping-Pong Club

"Quiet around here, isn't it?" Bill remarked, munching on a cookie.

"Unbelievably quiet," I agreed. It was January. Summer vacation was over. The children were back in school and Topper was down for his nap. Bill and I lingered over our afternoon tea chatting about this and that.

"Just think," I mused, "we have six children in school now. Jackie is so excited about going off with her big brothers and sisters every day, she wants to leave an hour early. Let's hope that feeling lasts. At the rate these kids are growing, it won't be long before Topper will be in high school looking like a proper Aussie in a gray shirt, short pants and knee hose."

"It's the wide-brimmed digger's hat that does it," Bill said with a chuckle. Then, on a more serious note, he added, "It doesn't seem to bother the boys, but I'm awfully glad I didn't have to wear a necktie to school when I was growing up."

"Me too," I echoed. "I don't think girls should ever have to wear them. I'm glad the primary school doesn't have that requirement. Can you imagine knotting neckties for three girls every morning!"

"No, I can't," he laughed. "I wouldn't want to carry a suitcase full of books every day, either. Mickey weighed his port the other day and it was twenty pounds."

"Wow, no wonder they're developing such broad shoulders. Carrying that much weight, a mile to the jetty and back, would have to be a great muscle builder."

Pouring fresh tea, I asked, "Have you noticed a difference in Rusty lately?"

"You mean his sudden interest in girls?"

"Yes," I sighed. "Bringing up toddlers is one thing, but raising teens is a whole new challenge. Merran and Rusty are 'on' again. Two years ago it was a crush; now it's puppy love."

Bill grinned. "Teens live for the moment and each moment is the most important one of their lives. But Rusty isn't so wrapped up with the girls that he's forgotten other things, like work, sports and fishing. He told me Bob Stockwell is rowing over this weekend to go fishing."

"Fair dinkum! It's hard to believe that Bob's mother allows him to row four miles across the water in a little dinghy. Rusty told me he's been doing that since he was twelve. Fishing is great for them but it doesn't solve Rusty's problem."

"What is Rusty's problem?"

"A few of the kids are playing ping-pong at the Parish Hall once a week. Rusty wants Merran to go, but her parents won't let her because there is no adult supervision."

Bill sympathized. "That's too bad; kids need to socialize. Except for an occasional dance, there's very little on the island that lets them do that."

"Hon, I have an idea!"

Bill set his tea cup down with a "what now" look on his face and quietly asked, "An idea?"

"Yes. If I volunteer to be the chaperone, perhaps Curtis and Daphne will let Merran come to the hall."

"Jolly good," he said, obviously relieved that it didn't involve him. "Why don't you ring Daphne while I clear the tea things away?"

When Rusty came home, I told him the good news. "Merran is allowed to play ping-pong at the hall."

"How did that happen?" he asked in surprise.

"Your mom offered to chaperone," Dad explained. Rusty turned to me with a big grin. "Wow," was all he could say.

Eventually, Monday evenings evolved into the "Teen Ping-Pong Club." They talked about an age limit and settled on sixteen and older. It was decided to invite teens from the RKLM islands (Russell, Karragarra, Lamb, Macleay). Merran suggested collecting weekly dues to be saved for an outing. Mothers of the teens showed their appreciation by providing refreshments each week.

"We had ten teens show up last night," I told Bill, a few weeks later. "I need to find some other things for them to do. There aren't enough ping-pong tables to keep them all busy."

"You could take some of our board games," Mickey suggested.

"Jolly good, why didn't I think of that?"

"Games from the Game Book would be fun, too," Skippy offered.

"Thanks for the ideas. I'll try them next week."

The Monopoly game, new to Australians, was a big hit. The checkerboard was a battleground on which champions rose and fell. When tempers began to heat up, I'd introduce one of the party games. Seeing who could push an unshelled peanut across the floor to a finishing line—using only a toothpick—turned testy tempers into roaring laughter. Typical teens, they told jokes and teased each other. Occasionally, Merran, who was learning ballet, brought her music and danced for us.

After a few months the club had collected enough money for a boat trip down to Southport on the Gold Coast. Given the tense situation on the island, I kept my fingers crossed, hoping all would go well. There was a rumor that Grosse, the "bad seed" who had a reputation for stirring up trouble, would do just that.

It turned out to be more than a rumor. His daughter, Wilda, only fourteen, demanded to go on the trip. She was well aware that only those over sixteen were eligible. To avoid a misunderstanding, I knew I had to talk to her parents. Reluctantly, I climbed their porch steps and knocked on the door. Her mother, whom I had never met, answered the door looking anything but happy.

"What do you want?" she growled.

"It's about Wilda," I explained. "I'm sorry, but she's not old enough to go on the teen trip—"

Before I could finish my sentence, she shoved me across the porch, spouting language that I wouldn't want my kids to hear. Since there was obviously no room for

The Ping-Pong Club

discussion, I turned—hoping I wouldn't be attacked from behind—and calmly left.

The next morning, Wilda showed up when the teens were getting on the boat. Without asking, she climbed aboard and sat down. When she refused to leave, I had no choice. I canceled the trip on the spot. Given Grosse's past actions, chaperoning his daughter was not a situation I wanted to be involved with.

The teens were disappointed but felt that I had done the right thing. They knew I respected the rules they had made. Mickey was only fifteen and would have liked to have gone, but I would not bend the rules, even for my own son.

When things simmered down from the "almost" boat trip, we quietly arranged an outing to Brown's pool. Mr. Jackson volunteered to take us down in his launch. The teens thoroughly enjoyed the day. The ping-pong club went on for a few more months until the Routledges moved to Stradbroke. With Merran gone, Rusty and Mickey lost interest.

Luckily, during this time, Skippy was wrapped up in other things that kept him busy such as competing for top place scholastically and doing well in sports. The year before he had been High-Jump Champion of Queensland. This year, when the seventh-grade, Victoria Point Cricket team came over to play the Russell Island team, he was one of the best bowlers. It was a great game. They won the match. Skippy was happy.

Rusty and Mickey were even happier. At the game, they learned of a high-school youth club. At school the next day, they were told that the club was having a dance. The idea of attending a dance on the mainland sounded like a grand adventure. After school, they broached the subject very carefully—testing the waters for a favorable reply.

"Mrs. Collins offered to let us stay overnight," Rusty said.

"The Collin's teens are going to the dance, too," Mickey offered.

There didn't seem to be any reason not to let them go. I visualized the typical Australian high-school girls I had seen at school functions. They dressed in school uniforms, with neckties and heavy black shoes. According to the rules, the uniform could be no shorter than the top of the knee. Hair must be tied back neatly and no makeup was allowed.

Surprisingly, the dance provided Rusty and Mickey with a more American-like experience. They came home the next day unhappy about the whole affair.

"You should have seen the girls' skirts," Mickey frowned, "they were really short."

"Mom, it was crook," Rusty said, "the teens were petting all over the place."

"And smoking, too," Mickey protested indignantly.

"Dad, the noise was awful," Rusty moaned, covering his ears. "You would have run out of the hall when you heard those amplifiers."

We sympathized with their sad introduction to the real world. After an interesting discussion on the pros and cons of modern teenagers, Mickey summed it up. In his opinion, none of the youth at the dance looked very happy.

From what I've seen in Australia and hear about from the States, parents are constantly pushing their children into living far beyond their natural level of maturity, an unfortunate choice that can only lead to frustration down the road. We were very proud of our boys for their insight.

The Ping-Pong Club

At the next meeting of the Country Women's Association, I told about their experience. "It's sad that the RKLM youth population is too small to support functions like the ones teens have on the mainland, but they do need to socialize." After a brief discussion, it was agreed that the association would sponsor a monthly dance on Russell Island. I rushed home with the good news. Rusty was thrilled. "Wait until I tell the others," he whooped.

Usually, family dances were held only a few times each year. Rusty and Mickey were old enough to attend on their own, but we took the other children two at a time as a special treat. Age was not a factor in choosing partners. Men gallantly waltzed through the traditional circle folk dances with little girls in their arms while grandmas often danced with little boys.

We were delighted to see Rusty and Mickey starting their social life, dancing with older women and little girls who needed a partner. When I realized how different things were in the States and on the mainland, I was thankful for Russell Island.

Having regular monthly dances filled the gap. The whole island turned out to enjoy an evening of socializing.

Chapter Four

Rainy Days

Down under we have cyclones instead of hurricanes. Seven of them sailed by us that year. The closest one was Dinah. It blew in the same day our friends from Mackay, 600 miles north of us, came to visit. No, it didn't wipe us off the map but the tail end caused a bit of concern.

"Tom Barfield called," I told Bill when he came in from his morning chores.

"Fair dinkum, how's Tom doing?"

"He's coming over to Fiddler's Green with Margaret! They brought their oldest son down to Brisbane to enter him in boarding school. I invited them to come over after Michael gets settled. Tom said they'll be here on the early boat tomorrow."

"Wonderful," Bill said, sitting down to his cuppa and biscuits, "we haven't seen them since we went up to Mackay for Christmas. Jackie was just a toddler then."

"Who?" Jackie asked, hearing her name mentioned.

I lifted her onto my lap and offered her a biscuit. "Uncle Tom, he's coming over to see us."

"I remember him," Pam said, crawling up on her daddy's lap, "we went on a long trip to his house. He had a swimming pool."

"You've got a good memory," Bill said letting her sip from his cup of tea.

When Tia and the boys heard the news, they were delighted at the prospect of seeing the Barfields again. We all went down to the jetty to greet them when the boat came in. It was a beautiful day and a great reunion.

Back at the house Bill and the boys took Tom on a tour of the farm. As I readied lunch, I noticed Margaret glancing nervously at the sky. "Looks as though we may crop a bit of weather," she mused with a concerned look.

By afternoon the clouds were growing darker by the minute. When the men returned, I suggested that they stay overnight.

"I wish we could," Margaret answered, glancing at Tom. "But we do have to get back to the mainland. Tom's not the sailor type," she joked, "I'm the one who was born with webbed feet."

I asked Bill to arrange for a boat to take them over instead of waiting for the regular ferry. He called Mr. Jackson, who warned it might be rough, but said that he would do it. To keep Tom's spirits up, Bill and I decided to travel across with them.

"Can I go, too?" Rusty asked.

"I'll take care of things here," Mickey offered. With that assurance we headed for the jetty.

Although the wind had picked up considerably, the trip turned out to be more exciting than dangerous. At least, that's the way I saw it. Bill and Rusty stayed up front with Mr. Jackson, while Margaret, Tom and I sat in the cabin chatting. The water was choppy and the boat lurched now and then, but we didn't hear any complaints from up front.

Finally, Rusty came back to the cabin to tell us Mr. Jackson was pulling in to the dock. "It's calmer now," he told Tom and Margaret, "but it may be tricky getting on to the jetty."

"We'll be all right," Tom promised him. Bill and Rusty went outside to hold the rocking boat against the jetty while Mr. Jackson helped the passengers off.

"It was a wonderful visit," Margaret waved as they headed for their car. With a sigh of relief, Mr. Jackson backed away from the jetty and turned the boat toward home. Both wind and waves had lessened. I stayed on deck watching nature perform, wondering why Bill and Rusty were asleep in the cabin.

At home over a cup of tea, I learned the real story of what happened during that trip. "It was spooky," Bill said. "Mr. Jackson was feeling his way across the bay. The inky darkness wasn't the problem. He's accustomed to that. It was the debris in the water that was dangerous. He kept his speed down and had his spotlight playing on the water all the time."

"Mom," Rusty interrupted, "the wind was churning the water into foam. We could hardly see anything. Suddenly, Mr. Jackson's light pin-pointed something careening toward us. He swung the wheel and veered sharply just missing the object." Rusty twisted his hands in the air to demonstrate the emergency.

"It was a dead cow," Bill said.

"A cow!" I was amazed. "Where did the cow come from?"

"The Logan River," Rusty educated me.

"Yes," Bill explained, "Mr. Jackson told us that in a storm like this one, the Logan River backs up into the farmlands at Redland Bay. The water rushes in so fast, it sweeps cows standing on the riverbank right into the water where they drown."

"Too right," Rusty said in awe. "After that, we strained our eyes trying to see both sides of the boat at once. Before we reached Redland Bay, we spotted more cows, lots of logs and other debris."

Bill frowned, remembering. "I reckon if one of those logs had hit us it would have made a hole big enough to sink the boat. It was pretty scary."

"Oh, my goodness," I breathed. "I didn't know it was that bad! You were so quiet. We had no idea what you were going through. In this case, ignorance was bliss. I'm so glad I didn't know the whole story until it was all over. I would have been a nervous wreck."

For a while no one spoke. We were thinking of what might have happened. Finally, I broke the spell by pouring hot tea and offering another round of cookies. "When we finish these, it will be time for a good night's sleep. We don't know what tomorrow will bring."

"Tomorrow" brought more rain. We didn't see the sun for a week. It was too wet to work on the farm. "What can we do?" was the daily cry. Mickey didn't ask. He was happy for an opportunity to replace his wall maps with pin-up posters of the newest cars. Now that he was in high school, studying cars and creating a dashing wardrobe was more important than creating buildings.

"I'm going to clean the chooken house," Pam said. She had inherited Tia's "chookens." Tia had combined the Australian word "chook" with the American word "chicken" and come up with "chooken."

"Can I take Topper with me?" she asked, putting on her raincoat. "He can carry the chicken feed." She and Jackie were at the stage of alternating between pulling each other's hair out or moving with the unison of New York's famous Rockettes. When Pam was at odds with Jackie she played with Topper.

"All right, but don't let him wander away."

"I won't," she promised.

I watched them as they walked down the steps hand in hand. Topper had become a sturdy three-year-old. Pam, almost four years older, was slender and petite. Oddly, she only weighed a few pounds more than he did.

"Now, what can I do?" Tia wailed, breaking into my reverie. I turned to see a sad-faced nine-year-old who cried easily. I reached for the calcium. A good dose of calcium does wonders. It's the best "happy pill" I've found for growing children.

I handed her the calcium and gave her a hug. "I'm glad you asked. Would you and Jackie like to help make some cookies?"

Her face brightened. "Lots of them? Like you do with Rusty on Saturdays?"

"That's right," I said, "dozens. Enough for next week's lunchboxes and afternoon snacks. Do you know where Jackie is?"

"Yes, she's doing homework."

"Who's homework?" I wanted to know, trying to hide a smile. Jackie had just turned six and was in the first grade. She had school well under control. Her favorite pastime was doing her "homework" and offering to help the big boys with theirs.

By the time Bill came home with the mail, dozens of cookies had been baked, cooled and stored in biscuit tins. "What's the news?" I asked setting out a sample plate of "bickies."

"Well, the CMF is going to invade the island." Like Mickey, Bill gives little tidbits bits of information. The rest is question-and-answer time.

"What is the CMF and what are you talking about?" I asked testily. After standing in the kitchen all morning I was not in the mood for games.

Sensing my frustration he explained, "The CMF, which means Civilian Military Force, is like the American National Guard. This year the CMF chose Russell Island for its annual two-week maneuvers."

"Bad timing," I frowned. "We've had too much rain."

After school, Mickey came home with more news. "There's beer on the island," he said in a disapproving tone.

Normally the only beer on Russell Island was a bit of home brew. "Whose beer?" I asked for starters.

"The CMF's! Lots of cases of beer were delivered on the barge and are stored in the old shed at the top of the jetty hill. Mr. Wilson says it's beer rations for the CMF. The people on the island don't like the idea."

"Well, Mickey," I explained. "It might be an Australian custom to provide a certain amount of beer for the troops.

Rainy Days

A long time ago, I read that the English used to provide a rum ration for their soldiers and sailors. They mixed it with water so the men would feel better but wouldn't get tipsy. Dad told me that America used to do the same thing."

"Too right," his dad said. "We were allowed five bottles of beer and Coke each week. I used to sell my rations and spend the money on movies." Mickey was not impressed.

I comforted him, "It will be all right.

Within a week two hundred troops landed on the island. It rained…and rained. Most of the time their vehicles were stuck in the mud, chewing the island roads into mires. Training exercises were held near Sliep's farm at the south east end of the island. The young boys were enthralled with a close-up view of army life. It was probably the most exciting thing that had happened on Russell for years.

When I heard that the CMF officers were invited to our Saturday night dance, I wondered if I should go. "Aren't you getting ready for the dance?" Bill asked.

"I don't know. I hate to miss it but I was thinking of the stories you use to tell me about your early Navy days. Do you suppose the beer rations will cause any problems?"

"We can always leave if things get rowdy," Bill promised. Encouraged, I dressed up as usual. More fashion conscious than most of the island women, I easily stood out in a crowd no matter what I wore. My purpose was to please Bill rather than others. "You look stunning," he approved when I was ready. A compliment like that always made the effort worthwhile.

Surprisingly, instead of the usual folk dances, the CMF had provided music for dances like the jitterbug, two-step and fox trot. I jitterbugged with the colonel and discussed world affairs with the other officers. I had worried unnecessarily. The officers behaved themselves like proper gentlemen.

On the way home, Bill told me that the island women had been casting looks of disapproval my way. "Oh dear," I moaned, "I forgot! Australian women don't mingle with men. I'm in trouble now."

"It's all right," he consoled me, "I enjoyed watching you have fun. We haven't been to a dance like this one since we left the States."

"Thanks, Hon," I said snuggling up close to him. "I really did have a good time. I wouldn't want to do this every week, but socializing with people from the mainland was a delightful change."

"We've been invited to the Chaplin's Field Mass tomorrow, do you want to go?"

"That would be interesting. What time does it start?"

"Six thirty," he said, waiting for my reaction to the early hour. I just moaned.

The mass was a unlike any service I had ever attended. There were no chairs. We all stood in an open field. Besides the troops and a few civilians, it was well attended by biting sand flies and hungry mosquitoes. I felt sorry for the men who weren't immune to our local insects. Just as the mass ended, God treated us to a beautiful sunrise.

By afternoon the troops were gone and the island had returned to normal. Well—almost normal. We were left with rain-soaked roads and bogged vehicles. Repairing the damage from heavy weight combat vehicles kept people busy all over the island, especially on the road to Canaipa at the southeast end of the island. For many days after the maneuvers, it took Ron Brown's three boys an hour of sloshing through mud and mire to get to and from the school boat.

It was a high price to pay for the CMF adventure but no one regretted the experience.

Chapter Five

The Power Cometh

With the excitement of maneuvers over, I needed something interesting to occupy six "semi" adults. "I think I'll have a sewing bee," I told Bill. "Keeping everyone in clothes is a challenge. I work from nine to five as a farmer and from eight to midnight as a seamstress. There is an incredible amount of things to make for a family of nine. I've been trying to find time to sew summer pajamas but other things keep getting in the way."

"So...," said Bill, putting my scattered pieces of information together, "you're going to get them done by teaching all the kids to sew?"

"Fair dinkum," I said, watching him shudder.

"Well," he smiled weakly, edging toward the door, "I've got some work I have to do out in the shed."

When the Routledges moved to Stradbroke, they sold us their treadle sewing machine. It was an ancient foot-operated Singer. One of the best $10 investments I ever made. After I figured out how it worked, I called the children together. "Who wants to learn to use this sewing machine? It's a lot of fun and all you do is rock your feet back and forth. Besides, you can sew without turning on the generator. I had one like this when I was growing up. Just think of all the wonderful things you can make." I paused. Mickey and Rusty rose to the challenge. I had done a good selling job.

"Tomorrow," I announced, "we're going to have a sewing bee. Do you all know what that is?"

"Yes," Skippy said, "it means everybody has to work."

"Jolly good!" I applauded, "And when we're done, you boys will have three pair of new summer pajamas with short pants!"

"Well," Skippy grinned, "at least we get something out of this."

That evening, I cut out all the pajama pieces and pinned them together. The next day, we moved the treadle sewing machine and my electric one into the living room. Jackie and Pam served as "carriers." They carried a pile to Rusty, who did the straight seams on the treadle machine. Then he tossed them over to me to do the curved seams on my machine. I tossed them on to Tia to remove the pins. The carriers took them to Mickey, who trimmed the seams. Then on to Skippy, who threaded elastic through the casings.

What a circus! When Bill came in with the mail, he was shocked to see pajama pieces flying through the air in every direction. Had his wife and children gone mad? I laughed at the relief on his face when he realized what we were doing.

It was a big job but we got it done. Afterwards, with great satisfaction, we rewarded ourselves with a plateful of cookies and a gallon of passion fruit punch. But most of all, I enjoyed the way the children cheerfully added sewing to their list of accomplishments.

With the pajamas out of the way, I decided to create a whole new wardrobe for myself. I could see great possibilities in cutting up dresses I made in Japan in 1959 and redesigning them for the rising hemline of the '60s. We didn't waste a thing around here. And now, I had a non-electric sewing machine to use when the generator was off.

We had struggled with that big diesel generator for three years. It was perched in a dark corner of the tin shed. We started it with a hand crank. Once it was going nicely, there was a little lever that had to be adjusted by hand. The trick was knowing when—too soon and the motor stalled, too late and it sounded as though it was going to blow up. I wouldn't even attempt to start it. The boys, braver than I, thought it was pretty scary too.

Stopping the beast was easier. We held the lever down until it coughed as though it was choking to death. If the boys were still up when I finished sewing at night, they killed it for me. But if it was really late—and with me, that was almost always—I'd wake Bill up to shut it off. If he and the boys were away, I'd take one of the girls with me for support. It made such a horrible loud noise inside that tin shed, an extra pair of ears waiting outside gave me a measure of security. For years, rumors had circulated about power lines being run across Russell to the sand mining industry on Stradbroke Island. If that ever happened, it would give us a possible chance of being hooked into the loop. Ah, sweet dreams!

And sometimes, dreams do come true. Bill brought the exciting news home with the morning's mail. "The electric company is dropping poles along the roads," he announced. Rumors were one thing, but poles were something solid to pin my hopes on. I felt another brilliant idea coming on.

"Hon." Bill, who had been reading the paper, looked up quickly. Recognizing the code word "Hon," he knew something big was about to be suggested. "Wouldn't it be a good idea to have our house rewired for modern electricity now? That way," I reasoned, "we'll be ready when it does come."

Bill thought for a minute. "I reckon so. That's a good idea. I'll call our friend, Ron Bachelor, in Clayfield." Ron agreed to come over on weekends to do the job. It proved to be a good move; ours was one of the first homes to be hooked up to the main line. After three years of promises, we were finally to have electricity!

After weeks of watching the poles go up and wires being strung, we received word that everything was ready. When the switch was thrown, pandemonium broke loose in our house. Bill warned the children not to plug American things into the wall sockets. "We still have to use the transformers for those," he explained. We all scattered in different directions. I was trying my electric sewing machine when Bill called from the dining room.

"Hon, come look. The freezer works!" For over three years, our huge Amana freezer had sat quietly in the corner of the dining room. We used it as extra pantry storage, but now we could freeze and store fresh food!

I reached in to feel the coolness. "Jolly good! But we had better get these things out. I don't want frozen ketchup and ice cold sugar."

The Power Cometh

"Mom!" Rusty called from the kitchen, "the mixer works! We can make ice cream and cakes whenever we want!"

I looked at Bill. "Speaking of ice cream, what about the fridge downstairs?"

"Righto! Hey, boys, let's change the refrigerators!" They took the kerosene fringe downstairs and moved the electric one up into the kitchen. "Don't forget to plug it into the transformer first," Bill cautioned.

We bought two of the greatest luxuries in the world, an electric water heater and an electric stove. What bliss! Hot water at any time! Dinner at a decent hour. Breakfast toast with an electric toaster. Lights, laundry, all at the flick of a switch.

I could stay up as late as I pleased, or get up in the middle of the night, without worrying about the generator. I could start the washer without waiting for Bill to turn the generator on. He was thrilled at not having to fill the kerosene refrigerator tank, clean the stove chimney or haul and saw wood. The children could play their records during the day. They could see to read in their rooms when the weather was dull.

But wait a minute—there was a price to pay for the blessing. When we moved to the island, the red dirt roads were canopied with huge eucalyptus trees. One never knew what might be up at the top of a hill, or in the next gully. It was hard to tell just how many people were on the island. Their farms were all privately tucked away behind a thick growth of flowering groundsel and pine trees.

To run the electric wires, a great swath of gum trees were cut down, leaving tree stumps, half-burned logs and rubbish. The island wasn't prepared to make beautiful front lawns a popular way of life. Usually, lawns were mowed just to keep snakes from getting into the house.

Now we could see almost a mile in each direction, but we really didn't want to. And, finally, we had land-grabbers selling off subdivisions on Macleay Island. Now that Russell had electricity, it would be the next plum.

Of course, other things were changing too. At dinner time, I complained about civilization taking away as much as it gives. With all our bright lights, I was seeing dirt and dust that I had never noticed before. "I spend more time cleaning and polishing than I have for years," I moaned.

"That's right," Mickey agreed, "and you notice every finger mark and all the junk in the corners of our closets."

"And..." Tia added, "you make us clean things that didn't use to matter."

I laughed. "I guess we're all missing the 'old' Russell Island."

"Yeah," Rusty waved his spoon for emphasis, "But I wouldn't trade the new for the old."

"Well spoken, " Dad said. "But we did trade something old for something new." He had their attention. "What?" everyone asked at once. Dad smiled. "We bartered with Ron and Jack: our wood stove and generator for their carpentry work. They'll be making new cupboards for the kitchen."

When everyone calmed down from hearing this news, Skippy introduced another subject. "What kind of ice cream are we having for dessert?"

"Banana nut, my favorite!" Pam said, heading for the kitchen.

"Let me help you," I offered, pushing my chair back, "things are a mess out there."

Renovations were already under way in the kitchen area. Bill had taken out the pantry and removed the wall between the kitchen and dining room. Ron and Jack were going to replace the wall with a breakfast-bar divider. I had designed it to have cupboards and drawers that could be opened from either side. When they arrived to begin work, Jack looked at the plans and said, "It can't be done."

I responded, "I know you will find a way." And he did! The finished product was wonderful. Three feet high, eighteen inches deep and five feet long. The children could set the table for dinner without dodging around us in the tiny kitchen. If we needed dishes in the kitchen, we didn't have to walk around to the dining room. Even the drawers were double-ended. They had handles on both ends. Jack did a great job.

While they were working on the kitchen, Bill removed the wall between the old dining room and the living room, giving us a spacious fourteen by twenty-five foot area. As he packed up his tools, my master builder remarked with satisfaction, "When you have bigger children, you need bigger rooms."

"It's wonderful," I praised. "It looks so bright and airy in here now. But look at those piles of books. What can we do with them? They're spread all over the house."

"I don't know," he said. "But I have a feeling you're going to tell me."

"Well..." I paused, trying to think of a way to make him delighted with a new building project. "Could you make a four-foot high bookcase along the living room wall between the bedroom doors?"

He looked at me as though I had lost my mind. "That would be twelve feet long," he frowned.

"Yes!" I said with eyes shining. "Jolly good! I'd love it!"

What could he say except "okay"? "But," he added, "you'll have to wait for the bedroom bureau and the door to your closet." He had just finished "his and her" closets in our bedroom, one on each side of the window. The door for my closet was ready to be hung, but the bureau was still under construction.

"That's all right," I smiled, picking up a pile of books, "you can finish the bedroom while I gather the rest of the books."

Most of our cupboards, shelves and closets had been built out of the enormous packing cases that brought our shipment from the States. Bill figured that between the pine boards and plywood sheets, we'd have enough lumber to rebuild the whole house, if we wanted to. Actually, that was what we were doing.

Chapter Six

The Pot Simmers

Although some people thought Jack Wynn was kind of cranky, we'd always gotten along well with him. Jack and I discussed the issues of life over our fence-line. I always admired how well his horses behaved. They never seemed to wander away. Perhaps that was because they were so mature. Big plow horses with big feet.

Naturally, it was a surprise when we received notice from Jack regarding *The Dividing Fences Act* of 1953. It was a form letter stating that he wanted us to join him in demolishing the existing fence between our properties and erecting a new one. It contained a threat of legal consequences if we failed to comply.

"What on earth is going on?" I asked Bill.

"I suspect Grosse has something to do with this," he said, shaking his head.

"Jack has been spending quite a bit of time over there lately."

"But he needs a fence like he needs a flock of geese," I protested. "I know what I'll do. I'll respond to his request." I grabbed my handy tablet and carefully composed an answer in my best legal wording. I presented it to Bill for approval.

> *Dear Jack,*
>
> *Since the nature of use of our property is for small crop farming, we feel that the present fence is sufficient and cannot authorize its destruction.*
>
> *However, if you care to raise livestock and desire a stock-proof fence you may, at your own expense, run wires along our fence posts.*
>
> *Sincerely yours*

Bill nodded with a smile. "You do have a way with words." He delivered the letter via the post office. Strangely, Jack seemed to lose interest in building a new fence. We heard no more on that subject. Unfortunately, it was the first of a steady stream of unpleasant situations—all tracing back to Leo Grosse. He and his "live-in" and three children were newcomers to the island. I called him a bad seed because trouble and strife were his close companions.

Tom Hamlin was the next one to do odd things. He came by one day representing the Road Committee. "I've come to collect the road tax," he announced.

"I didn't know there was such a thing as a Road Committee or a road tax," I said in surprise. "Why should I pay a road tax when I have to take my shoes off to go down to the community hall? Those volcanic stones are like walking on marbles. And where was the Road Committee when

Mickey had that bad accident riding his bike down the steep school hill? Nothing was done about the roads then." We chatted for a while about the condition of the roads. He left with our promise of a road tax payment when the roads had been improved.

Shortly, a grader was brought over from the mainland. A working bee was scheduled to turn the steep school hill into a gentle slope. "Do you suppose they did that just to get our road tax?" I asked Bill.

"Probably," he grinned. "At least we can all feel safer walking down to the hall and the jetty."

A while later, basking in his road success, Tom asked if we wanted to become co-owners of a car on the mainland. "We could leave the car in the parking lot at the Redland Bay jetty and take turns using it when we have business in town. I've already approached Ron and Jack with the idea and they're both interested."

Bill and I discussed the possibility during our evening walk. "It would be nice not to have to wait for the bus from Redland Bay every time we go to town," Bill mused.

"And another wait for the bus coming back from Brisbane," I said. "That's the hardest part. By then, I'm worn out from carrying packages all around town."

"Fair enough," Bill agreed. "We could stow the packages in the car. That would be a great help. If Ron and Jack are involved, it should be all right. We'll give it a go."

We told Tom, "yes." We all chose designated days of the week. The only rule was: Always leave the tank full of petrol for the next person. I've heard it said that joint ownership among friends never works out, and a year later I would have to say, "That is right."

It wasn't long before Tom forgot which days of the week were "his," "theirs" or "ours." He also forgot how to fill up the tank and allowed other people to use the car. Despite all that, the car was a boon and Tom's antics provided us with some laughs as well as frowns.

One day we went over on our designated day expecting to use the car. It wasn't there. "Oh dear," I fumed. "We'll be late for our appointment if we have to wait for the bus."

"There's not much we can do about it now," Bill said, shrugging his shoulders. "However," he added with resolve, "I intend to charge Tom for the expense of taking the bus into town. Perhaps that will help him become more responsible." It didn't.

Just before we used it for the last time, Tom told us he had done a valve job on the car. "It should run like a top now," he grinned.

We were almost to Brisbane when it quit cold—never to go again, according to the mechanic. "At least not without a complete overhaul," he said. We called a taxi and turned the keys over to Tom when we got home. It was his problem to solve. Needless to say, after that we were "strangers-when-we-meet."

Months later, Tom brought the car back to the island. He did a complete overhaul, without consulting us, and sent us an itemized bill. Bill queried the unauthorized repairs.

"I don't think it matters," I told him, "because once we divide the bill by three and subtract our taxi fares, there nothing left to pay."

Ron and Jack, obviously older and wiser, donated their share of the car to us. We offered to sell it to Tom and be done with the matter. He wasn't interested. Instead of returning the car to the mainland, he flaunted it on the island. "This is not right," I told Bill.

"I could put a rope on it sometime and tow it away," Bill suggested.

"Jolly good," I said. "If he is allowed to get away with this, no telling what that crowd will try next."

That idea didn't work either. The rope broke. "Never mind," I told Bill. "At least we made a statement: don't mess with the Moores."

Obviously shaken, Tom took the car down to the other end of the island. He removed the tires and put it up on blocks at a friend's house. It was several months before we heard he was planning to use the car again. "There must be something we can do to prevent that," I protested to Bill. "After all, we still own two-thirds of that car."

"There's not much we can do," he said.

"Yes, we can." I jumped up excitedly. "I have a plan!"

"What do you mean?" he looked puzzled. "There's no way I can move that car. They took the tires off and it's up on blocks."

"You don't have to," I said, "let me explain."

A few days later, all the islanders were occupied with the annual picnic over on Macleay. After breakfast, Bill took his hat from its peg and told me, "I'm going for a walk with the boys." I watched from the porch as they strolled down through the woods carrying gunny sacks. I knew what they were going to do.

It wasn't long before I heard them talking excitedly as they walked into the yard. I ran down the steps to meet them. Bill looked up with a satisfied grin. "The car has been evenly divided between its two owners. Come see what we have," he invited, as they headed toward the shed. Following them into the shed, I watched as they unloaded their gunny sacks.

"We tried to be very fair in dividing the car," Rusty explained.

"Righto," Skippy said, "that bloke owns the car and we own the generator, carburetor and distributor."

"Don't forget the fuel pump, spark plugs and wires," Mickey added.

I laughed. "That should put an end to the story of 'The Car Caper.' Let's go upstairs. I have cookies and milk waiting for you."

It did end "The Car Caper." No further mention of the car was heard on the island. But the poison of the bad seed continued to spread.

Grosse's arrival had changed the whole climate of our community. After moving into Sergio's place, he had quickly formed a drinking crowd that constantly changed, depending on whom he could mislead. Butch, the Paddens and the Briars, who used to be our friends, were very much involved. Sadly, so were many of the teens.

Until then, the only big drinkers on the island had been Butch and Al Skidmore. Before the beginning of Saturday night dances, Al would hide a bottle of homemade wine up in a tree. Between numbers he would step outside and have a little nip.

One night, when we were all dancing sprightly to "The Pride of Erin," Al was sitting on a chair, playing his violin. I noticed him leaning unusually far to the right. "Look at Al," I whispered to Bill. "I hope he doesn't fall over."

Oddly, as we watched, Al, still playing the violin, slowly settled on to the floor. Without missing a beat at the piano,

The Pot Simmers

Mrs. Wilson glanced at him and remarked dryly, "Al made too many trips to the tree tonight." Those close by nodded in agreement. The dance went on uninterrupted. The islanders were accustomed to Al's ways.

But Grosse was a different story. Tom Hamlin spent more and more time at his house but was soon replaced by another islander. It was like a game of chess with someone being checkmated and dropped every now and then. Even though Leo Grosse and the Moores had never been formally introduced, we seemed to be in perfect accord to ignore each other.

Well, ignore might not be the right word. Island gossip had it that Grosse was out to "bring us down," partly because we were Americans and partly because we were minding our own business and not worshiping at his feet. It was like an Alfred Hitchcock psychodrama that you never expected to be a part of. His dislike for Americans was rubbing off on others. Everyone who went into his house came out hating someone.

Ted Thomas, who used to be at the jetty early to help everyone unload, was now the Ted Thomas who practically ran people off the road to get to the jetty at the last minute. Instead of his usual manner of mumbling in the background at meetings, he began to explode down front. The changes on Russell Island were having a bad effect on others, too.

Bill brought the latest news home with the mail. Unloading his tucker bag, he announced, "Grosse's friendship with Mr. Wolfe is causing problems in the school. The Parents and Citizens Organization is beginning to feel the effect of the head teacher's lack of leadership."

I nodded as I glanced through the mail. "Mrs. Wilson told me that the Jubilee plans are a mess."

"They're still fighting," Bill grinned. "The P&C president, secretary and several others had a special meeting. Unplanned, unannounced and unofficial. They worked out plans to make big money at the Jubilee."

"Oh, how are they going to do that?"

"Well, they ordered five hundred handbills promoting a free lunch and beer stall. When the ladies learned about it at the regular monthly meeting, they were up in arms. They wanted to know how they were to prepare enough food when they had no way of knowing how many people would be attending. At the regular meeting it was voted on and passed, to recall the ad, but no one ever did."

"Well," I sighed, "with the underhanded methods that were used, I can see why they would be upset. I'm glad we decided to stay away from Parents and Citizens meetings for a while."

"Too right," Bill agreed. "It's a shame Grosse had to move to the island the year of the school's 50th anniversary. There'll be a lot of people coming from the mainland to visit old friends. And lots of others who just want a free meal. I pity the person who has to determine how much food to prepare."

Despite all the strife, the weather chose to smile on the celebration. The ladies of the four islands had done a formidable amount of work to satisfy the free-lunch promise. As boatloads of hungry people arrived, Mrs. Dickson organized the food area. She blocked visitors from the kitchen so they wouldn't distract the workers. Seemed like a good idea, but it needed a bit more thought.

By afternoon, the workers in the kitchen were like a hive of angry bees. Their friends from all over Queensland had traveled for miles to visit them. But watchdog Dickson guarded her kitchen barricade and wouldn't let the guests through. So much for free lunches and beer.

The budget, posted in the shop after the Jubilee, showed a huge profit. But the small print at the bottom stated that all due bills hadn't been received yet. Mrs. Briar, the treasurer, told me, "When the rest of the bills are paid they'll be lucky to clear a fraction of the amount mentioned." Shortly after the celebration, all P&C money was placed into one "general" account.

"No one will ever know the real outcome of the Jubilee funds," I told Bill. "What a clever way to cover up blunders. I can see now why it is so difficult to get anything done on this island. Jim and Connie Graham were great teachers and great leaders. I admire them for the stability they created while they were here. It's amazing how some people produce harmony and others produce chaos."

I couldn't have been more right. Just before Easter, Grosse bought two calves. "He's not tethering those calves," Bill told me a few days later. "He's letting them run loose. I suspect he's trying to cause trouble for us. I told him there's a poison weed in our fields and it could kill the calves."

It worked for a while but it didn't last long. Easter morning they were back on our farm trampling the crops. Bill went up to the field just as Marvin, who was the son of the woman Grosse lived with, came to get the calves. "Keep the cows tied up or I'll shoot them," he told Marvin. He didn't really mean it, but I hoped that Marvin believed he did. Even so, I knew this wouldn't be the end of the story. A bad seed bears bad fruit.

Bill checked with the authorities in Cleveland to see what our options were. He was told, "If a neighbor's cow strays onto your field and the neighbor makes no effort to take care of it, the cow may be impounded. A fee of $5 a day may be charged for feed and care."

The next time the cows were allowed to stray, Bill tied them to the fence and let Marvin know about the law when he came to get them. "You already owe me $10," he informed Marvin, standing in front of the calves. "Pay up and you can take them home; leave them and the fee goes up." Without a word, Marvin scurried back to tell Grosse.

This happened on the day the Catholic priest made his monthly visit. As usual, he came to Fiddler's Green for lunch, taught at the school and said mass at the hall after school. When it was time to leave for the boat, he told Bill, "The jetty is so close; don't bother to drive me down, I'll enjoy the walk."

None of us realized the surprise waiting at the jetty. Grosse and three of his stooges accosted the priest when he arrived. They accused him of being a cattle rustling accomplice of Bill Moore. They threatened to turn him over to the police. Father Brosnan was a big man and quite capable of taking care of himself. He smiled at his accusers, turned, walked along the jetty and climbed aboard the boat. The idea of a Catholic priest helping Bill to steal cattle was the "chuckle of the year" at the Cleveland Police Department.

Bill kept the cows tied for another day. The next morning they were gone. Somehow they found their way home and decided to stay there. We never saw them on our property again.

Chapter Seven

Catching Up

I'm the kind of person who likes life to be slow, steady, regular, scheduled, no changes or surprises. I like to make plans and carry out my plans uninterrupted. In reality, nothing could be further from this fantasy than what my life actually is. Trying to explain this in a long overdue letter, I was inspired to rhyme:

A Letter Writer's Lament

A note from Jim and Mary. I'll answer it today.
Soon as I've done the dishes and put everything away.
There's laundry to do, I must not sit,
Floors to sweep and dinner to get.
A thousand carrots to be peeled and frozen.
My back is numb and my wrist feels broken.

Tomorrow for sure I'll drop them a line.
Just floors to scrub, there'll be plenty of time.
Uniforms to iron and a small pile of mending,
The jobs to be done seem never ending.
Hair cuts, shampoos, styles for the girls,
Plaits and ponytails and a few little curls.
Next week, for sure, I'll have time for that letter,
There's not much to do, things will get better.

Sunday it's quiet and with a bit of good luck,
A note I'll be sending before this month's up.
Who's outside shouting with a voice that is hoarse?
Topper ran through the laundry and hit the clothes hoist?
Five stitches this time, above the right eye.
I don't even panic, I've just strength to sigh.

The days have gone by one at a time.
The floors and the windows have all had a shine.
From carpets to ceiling I've done my best.
Surely I'm due for one day of rest.
My work is all finished. I look back with chagrin,
I've hurried on through in time to begin!

I read the poem through again. Did I do all those things? No wonder I have a never-ending "to do" list. I poured a cup of coffee, grabbed my pen and paper and headed for the gazebo. If I can't see what needs to be done I won't be tempted to do it. I promised myself, today is letter day. I climbed up into the gazebo, settled into the comfy cushions and began to write. But not for long—I wrote of the interruption…

Dear Jim and Mary,

I was just sitting down to write when the fellow next door started a fire in his field. He knew full well that a high wind was blowing in the direction of our woods. Rusty and I worked to hold it at bay until Bill and the other boys came home to help. There's not much that can be done when it's this dry. We lost a lot of trees but were able to save our irrigation plant.

1967 has been quite a year. Our peaceful island community disintegrated when a jealous neighbor started a wave of anti-Americanism. We took the girls out of the island school and sent them to school on the mainland with the boys.

If we're going to live here, Bill says, it's important not to become embroiled in the constant strife that's going on. There are several families on the island who keep very much to themselves. We've often wondered why—now we know.

We have four friends left, a shattered reputation and assurances from the police that they will rush over in their crash boat if a riot breaks out. Chief Constable Kitchen tells us we have a nice fat dossier on file at the police station. We consulted with several government officials who feel that the root cause of our problem is harvesting a successful crop and getting a bad neighbor at the same time.

Even though it's been a difficult year, our harvest, the best since we started farming, restored our confidence and allowed us to catch up on some very important needs. We bought a 1960 Holden station wagon. A bit of a rust heap but what a blessing. Four new tires, lots of body putty, a bit of tin, fresh paint and it looks like, if not new, at least close to it. We keep it on the mainland for trips to town.

Next we bought a piano. Tia, Mickey and I started on the road to musical greatness together. But even though they're greater, I'm lasting longer. The only time I get thoroughly discouraged is when they sit down and play at random everything they've ever learned—from memory. I'm still plodding along with sheets of music.

Bill's big purchase was a welder. Not particularly interesting but necessary on a farm. At least he was able to repair the tubular steel bunk beds that we had propped up on four-gallon milk tins and chunks of wood. Big boys can be pretty rough on bunk beds.

Another great improvement was enclosing the front porch. Painted yellow with white curtains, it provides a bright sunny background for our dark living room. We call it the "sun room"—a perfect place for the children to do their crafts.

When the Routledges moved we bought their plastic lounge suite. The first sofa and chairs we've ever owned. Up until Bill retired, the Navy supplied our needs at each duty station. With new furniture and drapes, the living room looks very nice. The bathroom and kitchen and dining room glow with new lino, paint and curtains. What a difference! We really feel like millionaires.

Just about the time we finished these improvements, my old washing machine went up in smoke. We replaced it with an inexpensive wringer type in hopes that one day—when we get water pressure—I'll be able to use my automatic washer. In the meantime, I feel more secure in the laundry than I have for years. We are thrilled to have electricity on twenty-four hours a day. What a difference it makes in daily living!

With all three girls in school, Topper is the only one at home during the day. He seems to be stronger and sturdier than the others were at his age. Since he turned three he comes to me less and less to be loved. For a week or more, he practically broke my neck with super-squeezes all day. I guess he was saying goodbye to toddlerhood. Now he cuddles morning and evening. The rest of the day he is busy-busy, learning and growing. Tia and I miss our "baby."

A few weeks ago he was outside looking for ways to help his brothers with their work. He picked up an axe that had just been sharpened. Before Skippy could caution, "Don't play with that Topper," it was too late. They looked on in horror as blood spurted out of a severed vein. It only takes a misguided moment for an accident to happen.

Bill scooped him up and carried him into the house while Mickey applied pressure to Topper's foot to stop the flow. Inside, they called for "nurse Mom" to perform first aid. My standard procedure is to stop the flow of blood, find out what happened, apply antiseptic to a clean damp cloth and tape it onto the wound. With calm soothing words, I prepared the patient for a trip to the mainland while Bill called to arrange for a boat.

Mickey went along to help at Redland Bay. Fortunately, we had the Holden for transportation. They were able to drive right to Cleveland where the doctor closed the cut with eight stitches. It turned out to be good practice for Mickey.

Three weeks later, as the poem says, Topper ran through a blanket hanging on the clothesline and hit the center post. This time Bill was away, so big brother Mickey took control. He knew just what to do. He called for a boat while I prepared the patient. Skippy went along as helper. When they reached Redland Bay, Mickey drove to Cleveland. This time it was five stitches just over his eye.

It would have been quicker and easier if I had the ability to stitch wounds. That's what Bill—thinking ahead—wanted me to learn before we came to Australia. "You can do everything else," he said.

I retorted, "No thank you! I'll clean the house, sew the clothes, cook the meals, cut the hair, but that, I will not do." Now, I spend my weekends clutching the aspirin bottle and running at every scream. Just don't ask me to stitch wounds.

Goodness, I didn't mean to go on so. The real purpose of this letter is to invite you and your family over to Fiddler's Green for a barbecue next weekend. We'd love to catch up on what you've been doing.

Jim and Mary did make it to the barbecue. They were delightfully impressed with the changes in our house and farm. "You've come a long way from the comic-opera farmers of a few years back," Jim joked. "What are you going to do next?"

"Connie wants to build a swimming pool," Bill grinned, glancing at me.

"Well," I said, defending myself. "I think it's better to make special memories for our children now, than to leave them with only money when we're gone."

"I agree," Mary said. "Where are you going to put the pool?"

"Right over there by the eucalyptus tree," I said with confidence, not realizing the time between wanting a pool and actually getting one is not written in cement.

Chapter Eight

Moving Dirt

"There's a bulldozer on the island," Bill announced, unloading his tucker bag.

"Oh," I said, leafing through the mail, "what about it?"

"We can hire it," he said.

"What for?"

"The swimming pool."

Now he had my attention! "Fair dinkum! It's been so long since we talked about a pool, I had forgotten."

Delighted with his surprise, he explained, "We don't have time to do the pool right now, but I thought it would be a good idea to get the area dug while the dozer is here."

"Jolly good." I gave him a big hug.

A few days later the dozer lumbered into the yard. It scooped out a 40x60 foot hole, four feet deep, between the two big gum trees down in the back yard. A perfect place for our future swimming pool—as soon as we found time to build it. And who knew when that would be.

From the kitchen window, I gazed at the area trying to visualize kids in bathing suits splashing in cool, clear water. The big pile of dirt that the bulldozer had pushed up to make the hole kept spoiling my reverie.

"That needs to go somewhere," I mused aloud, "but where?" Then it occurred to me that our house block was on a gentle slope and had no level area for games or a tennis court. *"Since tennis is an important sport in Australia, and the children are getting older,"* I reasoned to myself, *"we should have a tennis court."* The problem was, how long would it take me to convince three strong boys and one strong man to move the amount of dirt it would require?

I skipped down the stairs to have a closer look. Just then, Bill passed by on his way to the well. "Hon," I stopped him, "wouldn't it be great for the kids if we had a tennis court?"

Hon looked at me. I could tell he hoped this was just a nightmare and he soon would wake up. "Where would we put a tennis court?" he asked cautiously.

"We could put it out there, beyond the garden by the gum trees." I pointed to a field of tangled growth. It had a path worn through it. The path led to the road that went up the hill to the well. That was all we used it for.

"But it's not level," he said hoping to end this crazy idea.

"Well... why can't we take that pile of dirt the dozer pushed up and put it over there to make it level?" Women may not be logical, but they can be practical.

"Do you know how long that would take?" He picked up the petrol can and started off. "I've got to get this petrol up to the well before the pump stops," he said, over his shoulder.

"All right," I murmured watching his retreating back. "I'll do it on my own, just like the little red hen." And... I did. Some of it, anyway. Every afternoon, after I had dinner on the stove, I went down to the paddock armed with a shovel and our great big metal wheelbarrow. I started dig. Even though it took all my strength to push the barrow when it was full, I managed to move one or two loads before I went up to finish dinner.

One afternoon, Rusty came along while I was shoveling dirt into the barrow. "What are you doing?" he wanted to know.

"I'm making a tennis court," I told him.

He looked at me strangely and laughed, "A tennis court!"

"Yes, don't you think it would be nice to have one at Fiddler's Green? I'm going to move this pile of dirt over there to make it level." Glancing at him, I threw another shovelful of dirt into the barrow. "Then we can top it with ant bed. That's how they do it in Australia."

He sighed. Rusty knew his mother well. "Do you want some help?" he asked.

"Yes, that would be wonderful!"

He got a shovel from the shed. We worked together until I had to go back to the kitchen. After that, every afternoon on his way back from the fields, he stopped to help with a couple loads of dirt. It wasn't long before Mickey joined us. Both of them moved a few extra loads when I went in to get dinner on the table.

Then Bill, feeling guilty and outnumbered, joined the crew. It was a little bit here and a little bit there, like my grains of sand.

"You know what?" Bill said one night at dinner.

"What?" I asked.

"We're going to need a retaining wall to make that tennis court level."

"How can we do that?" I asked, happy that he was getting interested.

"I don't know," he said. "It needs to be strong. Cinder blocks would do it, but that's an awful lot of money. They would have to be sent over from the mainland."

"Isn't there a way we could make some?" Rusty asked. "After all, we've made everything else."

"Fair dinkum!" I exclaimed. "Hon, do you remember that block-making frame we saw in a catalog the other day? It makes blocks, bricks and flagstones. If we had one, we could make all sorts of things."

"That's a thought," he said. "Let's look at it."

I ran to get the advertisement. It showed a steel frame that made twelve 4x10 inch blocks at a time. "It says here," I read, "pour cement mixture into the frame, tamp down firmly. Lift the frame and let the blocks dry in the sun. The frame can be adjusted for solid bricks, split blocks or flagstones. It says you can even color the blocks, just mix dye with the water," I smiled, sure that he couldn't pass up such a deal.

"Go ahead and order it," Bill said. "I'll find some sheets of plywood to put the blocks on to dry."

The work involved wasn't quite as simple as the ad suggested. To find the right kind of gravel, Bill had to haul trailer loads from the other end of the island. The cement and gravel were mixed by hand in our big wheelbarrow. My job was adding buckets of water while Bill and the boys stirred the mixture. It was hard labor but, little by little, with everyone working together we had the blocks we needed.

Once the blocks were dry, we built a two-foot-high wall the length of the future pool area. The next thing we needed was a roller to settle the dirt and smooth the area. Fortunately, Curtis Routledge had offered Bill his roller when he moved. "Take it," he said, "you can keep it." Bill thanked him and pushed it behind the shed, never expecting to have any use for it.

While we were wondering what to do, Rusty ran behind the shed and came back trundling the roller. "Fair dinkum!" Dad exclaimed. "I had completely forgotten all about that roller. Here, let me give it a go." With everyone, except me, taking turns, the ground was settled and evened. I served as the cheering section, a much easier job. To have four strong males working for you is something really worth cheering about.

The next step was ant bed. In Australia ants build above ground rather than underground. They build ant beds that are three or four feet high. Broken down and crushed the ant bed makes a firm surface almost like cement. Bill and the boys roamed the top acres of our property and collected all the ant beds they could find. Crushed and rolled smooth, there wasn't enough for a grass-free surface, but at last we had a large flat playing area. Perfect for tennis.

"Besides tennis, this would be a great place for croquet," Mickey suggested, as we lobbed tennis balls at each other.

"You're right, but I don't like the Australian croquet sets. I doubt if we could find an American one here."

"Maybe we could get Aunt Betty to send one over," he suggested, glancing sideways to see how I'd react to the idea.

"Jolly good," I agreed. "I bet she would. I'll ask your dad."

It took a few months for it to come from the States, but when the croquet set arrived, it was a big hit with everyone. A great game for entertaining at parties and barbecues, or just to relax—especially from the frustration of planting.

Last year's planting went along swiftly but this year, even with our super planting system, it was a grind. The weather was dry and the water table way down. We could only plant and irrigate about five rows at a time. So far only half the total crop had been planted. We were doing tedious work that could have been be finished off in a couple of weeks with a few heavy showers or a good supply of water.

Hot and dusty after a morning of shifting irrigation pipes, we climbed the stairs to the cool of the house. The well had pumped dry and needed a while to recover. I hung up my work clothes and stretched out on the dining room floor. The best place to be on a hot day. Houses on stilts, with wide verandas, have natural air conditioning from the shade underneath: a blessing when the outside temperature is over 100 degrees. "Wouldn't it be great, if we had one of those really deep wells," I sighed.

"I was thinking the same thing," Bill said, stretching out beside me. "Perhaps our well has silted up over the years and the spring that feeds it is blocked. I could try to dig it deeper."

"You could do what?" I said, sitting up quickly. He had my full attention. "How deep is the well, anyway?"

"It was listed as sixty feet when we bought the property."

"Sixty feet!" I said doubtfully, flopping down again. "That's awful deep. I'm not sure I want you to do that."

"It'll be all right," he assured me, "I'll climb down into the well. You lower a bucket for me to fill. Then you and the boys pull it up. I'll rig a block and tackle to make it easier. And I won't stay down very long at a time. There isn't much oxygen at that depth, anyway."

I could see that he had made up his mind. "About the only time we can do it is on Sunday after the barge goes," I reminded him.

"That will be okay. It's cooler up there. The kids can go with us and play in the woods."

He rigged up a pulley system and let us know he was ready to dig. I dreaded the thought of Bill way down there in that little five-foot-square space all alone. For me, our afternoons at the well were tense nail-biting sessions. Fortunately, Bill could only stay down for short periods. He thankfully kept his promise to do just a little at a time.

It wasn't all bad. I took snacks and drinks for a treat. The kids had fun playing in the woods while we worked. We called these afternoons our "Sunday recreation" time. In a few weeks, we managed to deepen the well about three feet. It was a big job, but the children playing around helped diffuse the stress.

"I think we'll aim for a total of five feet," Bill announced one Sunday as he started the long climb down the ladder. The boys and I were ready and waiting to pull up the first bucket when Bill's head suddenly popped up and he climbed out. He face was chalk white.

"What's the matter?" I asked in alarm.

"There's a snake down there. I don't know how I got down past it. I was about to move my hand down to the next rung and there it was! Coiled around the rung, the snake was staring me right in the eye. It was too dark to tell if it was a deadly snake or not. In times like that, you don't hang around for more information. You move—and move I did! I must have climbed right up past it. Or maybe it was as scared as I was and decided to go the other way. I don't know, but here I am. Thank God."

"Gosh, Dad," Rusty breathed, "Australia has more poisonous snakes than any other country. You're lucky it didn't get you."

"You're not going back down there, are you?" I was horrified.

"Not today," he said.

He did go back down for a few more weeks with no mishaps. We worked until the well was sixty-five feet deep. It didn't improve the water supply that much, but it added a lot of new, white hairs to my growing collection.

Chapter Nine

Changes

The girls had been tucked into bed. Topper was settled for the night and the boys were busy with their homework. Outside, a brilliant white moon beckoned to us. "Do you want to go for a walk?" Bill asked.

"Yes, wonderful! Let's go visit Ron and Jack. A three-mile walk will do me good." By the time we were on the main road we had shed the cares of the day. Inhaling a deep breath of clean, fresh air, I reached for Bill's hand. "It's this time of night that makes the whole day worthwhile," I murmured.

"I know," Bill said, looking up at the bright sky. "It's so quiet and peaceful." Hand in hand we walked down the road. Our eyes and ears had become accustomed to the night's shapes and sounds. We seldom needed a flashlight to guide us anymore.

"Do you realize," I asked, "that another year is almost over?"

"Never gave it a thought. Just can't get used to a year ending during the summer."

"How about Halloween in the spring? With the situation as it is on the island, I'm wondering what to do about Halloween this year."

"I don't think it would be wise to rent the hall for a big party," Bill advised. "Someone is bound to cause trouble."

"Mmm, you're right. Mickey and I were talking about inviting just their friends from the mainland. He said Ron and Jack had offered to put some boys up if they stay overnight. We could have the girls at our house."

"Sounds like a good idea to me. I'll set up the barbecue and we'll have a cookout. I'm sure you and the kids will come up with some great entertainment."

"Jolly good, I'm glad that's decided. Here we are at Ron and Jack's!"

Sipping one of Jack's famous cups of coffee, we chatted about the island news. "Did you know that Vellensworths have sold their store?" Ron asked.

"No, who bought it?"

"Fred Hanes. He's the young electrician who came over to wire some of the houses when the power came on. He has already installed electricity in the shop and is planning to sell ice cream."

"The kids will love that," Bill said. "I'd walk a mile any day for an ice cream."

"What are you talking about," I chided, "you get ice cream for dessert every night. The best in town."

"Yeah, but going to a store and buying a cone is different," he grinned.

I reached for another cookie and changed the subject. "How will this sale affect the Wilsons?"

"Chris says he'll keep the post office and the phone service," Ron told us while Jack refilled our cups. "By the way, did Jack tell you about Bill and Gladdy Wright?" We shook our heads. He continued, "The Wrights used to have a grocery shop not too far from our store in Wollongong. They've just retired and will be coming over to look at a farm on Canipia Road, down near Brown's. They're good friends of ours. We want you to meet them when they get here."

On the way home we talked about the changes on the island. I asked Bill, "Have you heard that the Slieps sold their place and will be moving to Victoria Point? A development company is supposed to build a motel on their property."

"That's right, and there's going to be another small development just a mile from where we keep our boat. The area for a park has already been leveled."

I sighed, thinking of the changes. "I just don't get out enough to keep up with what's going on. It will seem strange not to have the Vellensworths in the store. They've been so helpful to us over the years."

"I guess change is the only thing that we can be sure of," Bill philosophized.

"You're right about that," I said. "Our next change will be the Halloween party. It's going to be far different from parties of the past. We need to come up with some ideas, and I know just where to go for some of the best."

"Where?" he asked. It was a loaded question.

I laughed. "From the kids, of course!"

The next night at dinner, I introduced the subject. "What are we going to do for our Halloween party this year?"

"You said we could invite our friends from the mainland," Tia reminded me.

"That's right, but what are we going to do when they get here?"

"Build a bonfire," Skippy suggested.

"That's not a bad idea," Dad said. I'm going to make a pit with our leftover blocks. We can build a bonfire in that, and when it burns down we can use it for the barbecue."

"What will you cook the stuff on?" Rusty, the practical one, asked.

"I've been thinking about that," Dad said. "I can take one of the round disks off the disk plow and lay it across the top of the pit."

"Perfect," I applauded. "Now, what are we going to cook?"

"Hamburgers," they chorused.

"Okay, we can have potato salad, beans and chips with the burgers."

"Excuse me," Mickey interrupted, "isn't it going to be pretty dark outside? It's only springtime, you know."

"Christmas lights!" Pam shouted.

"Silly," Jackie poked her, "it's not Christmas."

"Wait a minute," Dad put up his hand. "Mom, don't we have some strings of large bulbs?"

"Yes, quite a few of them, I think. Since we haven't had any power, they've been packed away for years."

"Well, if they work, I could string them across the yard to the shed. It would be a good place for the picnic table and we could see what we're eating."

"Wonderful. Now all we need are the games."

"I'll find some in the game books," Rusty offered.

"Skippy, Topper and I can help get things together," Mickey volunteered.

"And we'll help Mom with the cake and cookies," Tia pronounced, looking at Pam and Jackie.

"Mom! Mom! Can we make cupcakes with pumpkin faces?" Jackie asked.

"And big paper ghosts," Pam beamed.

It was a wonderful party at Fiddler's Green. We entertained a half dozen boys and girls from the mainland. They were thrilled to come to the island for an overnight stay. We played racing games, laughing games and team games. After dinner the kids roasted marshmallows and told ghost stories under the stars. We had gotten through another holiday without any unpleasant incidents. I hoped things were settling down. But that was not to be.

A few weeks later Mickey came rushing in from school. "Mom!" he exclaimed, "guess what? We have a new store!"

I started the twenty questions. "Where, Mickey?"

"The Wright's have bought the old fertilizer shed on the top of the hill, just before you go down to the jetty. They're going to make it into a store for their daughter to run. I told them I'd help them," he grinned. Nothing could have excited him more than a new store within walking distance. A dream come true.

It was wonderful news but I needed further information. "Is that building really big enough for a store?"

"Fair dinkum, Mr. Wright told me it's 20x30 feet. He's going to partition the back part for an office and storage room. Gladdy said they're going to have trays slanted to display items. They will be getting their supplies from a warehouse in Brisbane."

Trust Mickey to get all the details, I thought. "Gladdy?" I questioned with raised eyebrows.

"Yes," he explained sheepishly, "she asked us to just call her Gladdy."

"Well, if she asked, I guess it's okay."

"She said everyone calls her Gladdy. She likes it that way," he assured me.

Every afternoon on his way home from school, Mickey stopped to see how the renovations were going. He loved watching the building progress and asked numerous questions about running a store.

One day he came home with a question. "Don't you think they should have a sign for the store? If it's just a building how will people know it's a store?"

"Perhaps we could make a sign as a welcome gift," I suggested.

"I'd be glad to cut the plywood if you and Mickey will do the painting," Bill offered.

The project was on. Bill cut a 2x3 foot board and Mickey painted it white. When the paint was dry I printed "Ann's General Store" in big green letters.

"Now, everyone will know there is another shop on the island," Mickey exclaimed proudly. He took the sign down to the shop and helped Mr. Wright put it up.

Gladdy stocked the store with things you need when you really need them—wonderful products such as silk stockings, toothbrushes and food staples. Unless you've lived on an island, you can't appreciate buying nylons without having to take a boat and bus to town. Gradually, she included gift items for the children and little toys that they could buy with a few cents. She had a talent for finding out what people would be inclined to buy and then providing it. Of course, a new store on the island wasn't allowed to just slide in. Some people can't tolerate competition.

We had been getting our bread from Mr. Hanes' store. Each morning, the Redland Bay Bakery sent the day's orders over in a breadbox. Usually, each loaf was wrapped in newspaper upon purchase. Mr. Hanes wasn't wrapping the bread at all. For this, and for several other reasons, we began to buy our bread and many other things from Ann's Store.

Apparently, this upset Mr. Hanes. He chose the bread delivery to bring us back into line. He told the bakery not to supply us through Ann's Store. The bakery sent me a note to that effect. I sent a note right back:

> *Having our bread handled through Ann's General Store is an arrangement we consider quite satisfactory. In the past, we have found Mr. Hanes to be unreliable. I believe he is aware of our feelings, which is why he approached you rather than came to us.*
>
> *As one of your first and most satisfied customers on Russell Island, we are pleased to tell our friends of your excellent products and service. However, if you find the present manner of delivery inconvenient, perhaps we can make arrangements elsewhere.*

After the bakery received my note, there was no difficulty in our bread service. They continued to send us their delicious, unsliced, double loaves of whole wheat bread through Ann's General Store. Bill or the kids brought them home nicely wrapped in sheets of newspaper.

During all of this the Wrights became our good friends. Mr. Wright was very quiet. Gladdy was inclined to scold him constantly. Her favorite word was "Beeelllll," her voice growing shriller as she stretched the word out. Actually, I don't think Bill minded being scolded. Folks gave him a lot of sympathy because of it.

Not at all dumb, he had a way of getting back at Gladdy by "forgetting" to do something that was important to her. Like forgetting half the items on her shopping list when he went to the mainland warehouse.

One day, while Bill was loading produce onto the barge truck at the jetty, Topper and I walked up to the store to say g'day. Topper announced his purpose right away. "I have a penny," he grinned, holding up a coin. "I want some bubble gum or a lolly, please."

"Oh, love," Gladdy moaned, "I feel so crook. There isn't any gum—or lollies. Mr. Wright forgot to bring them from Brisb'n. I had them on me list." Looking at me, she apologized, "I just don't know what I'm going to do. He forgets half the things I order."

The look of disappointment on Topper's face inspired me to make an offer. "We're going over tomorrow. Could we pick up some things for you?"

"If you wouldn't mind," her face brightened, "t'would be a blessing."

"Not at all. Since we now have a car on the mainland, it would be no problem."

She gave me a list and treated Topper to a cupcake. We chatted until Bill finished loading. Hearing the tractor chugging up the hill, we waved g'day and climbed into the empty trailer.

At home, I told Bill about the problem and of my promise. "That's fine for this week," he said, "but what will she do when we aren't going to town?"

"How about Mickey?" I suggested. "He drives and would love to go shopping. It's his favorite pastime."

"That sounds like a good idea. He does love to shop. We'll mention Gladdy's plight when he comes home from school."

That evening we discussed the possibility with Mickey. "Yeah, sure," he agreed. "I'd like to do something for the store and for Gladdy. She's been good to me."

Gladdy's biggest asset was a heart of gold. She was always kind and thoughtful, especially with the children. When Mickey told her he would be able to pick up things in Brisbane for her, she was delighted. It was much less stressful to have Mickey do the shopping than to scold her forgetful husband.

Chapter Ten

A Boat to Float

"Guess what," Skippy said, dropping his port by the door.

"Put your port in your room and come tell me your news," I said, setting out cookies and milk. After-school snack time was news time. Since the girls were going over to the mainland school with the boys, they all came home at the same time. The rest of the crew would be pouring through the door at any moment.

"Hey, Mom!" Mickey, next to arrive announced. "Gladdy has a cousin!" In the interest of fairness, I told him to put his things away first.

"He's a horse trainer," Skippy said with awe, grabbing a cookie and sitting down. "I wish I could do that," he mumbled around a mouthful of oatmeal cookie.

Tia and the girls ran up the steps and burst in the door. "We know a cattle drover!" they shouted together. Before they could drop their ports, I pointed to their bed rooms. When everyone settled down, I began to sort the information. "How many people are we talking about?"

"Just one, Gladdy's cousin, Gerard McGee," Rusty said, arriving on the scene with Topper on his shoulders. "He comes from Warwick about sixty miles northwest of us," he said, handing Topper a cookie.

Skippy gulped down his milk and added, "He brings shipments of cattle down to Brisbane. He said he'll come over to visit Gladdy whenever he has time—"

"He was there when we went to pick up the bread," Mickey interrupted. "He likes kids. He said he has lots of nieces and nephews."

Gerard McGee was a bachelor in his fifties. He had a dry sense of humor, delivered with a twinkle in his eye. Gradually, between droving jobs, he spent more and more time on the island, helping Gladdy at the store. The day I stopped by to meet him, he was busy rebagging wholesale items into small packages. "He's like a gift from heaven," Gladdy declared.

"What a blessing! We could use one of those," I joked.

"Just call on me," Gerard drawled with a shy grin. "I'd be mighty glad to help whenever I'm on the island."

And help he did. If we needed an extra hand on the farm, he was always there. He worked with Bill on heavy jobs when the boys were in school. He was full of wisdom and know-how, a special friend when our island friends were few. He and I enjoyed discussing the deep issues of life over a cup of tea such as the greatness of God and the problems of the world—my two favorite subjects.

A Boat to Float

There were other friends we were getting to know on the mainland. The *Seagull* had become an important part of our lives. Our newly-renovated launch gave us freedom to come and go on our schedule.

Best of all, it allowed us to travel across the bay to Cleveland for special affairs at the children's schools. Unfortunately, these events often fell during the spring rainy season, especially the November Fancy Dress Ball. The Fancy Dress Ball is a cousin to America's Halloween costume parties. It was one of the biggest events of the year.

We made plans for the children to stay with friends after school so they didn't have to go home on the boat and come right back to the ball. "What about our costumes?" Tia asked. "They won't fit in our ports."

"Dad and I will bring them over on the *Seagull*," I assured her. "I still have a bit of sewing to do, but they will be there in time for the ball."

"Goody," Pam grinned, shouldering her port and heading for the door.

Skipping down the stairs, Jackie called back, "Don't forget the costumes."

That afternoon I finished sewing while Bill worked on the boat. I wasn't sure what he was doing, but he had mumbled something about putting the bilge-pump drain in a new location.

With my eye on the clock, I packed up the costumes wondering what was keeping him. Dressing Topper, I heard him running up the stairs. "Sorry I'm late," he apologized, hanging his work clothes on a peg. "I'll be ready in a minute."

I gathered the things we needed to take and we began our usual routine: load everything onto the truck. Drive to the jetty. Load everything onto the trolley. Push the trolley to the end of the jetty. Transfer everything to the boat. Park the truck and board the boat. As we went through the motions, I thought wistfully of people who live on the mainland. *Their life is so simple*, I thought, *just put things in a car and drive off.*

Well, out into the bay, I noticed a three-inch hole where the old bilge drainpipe had been. "Hon," I inquired, "did you know this hole hasn't been covered?"

"Yes," was his terse answer.

"Is it safe?" I persisted. "It's only about five inches above the waterline."

"It will be all right," he assured me. The bay is calm and the boat isn't rocking."

I sat watching the hole. I wondered how far I could swim if the boat sank. Suddenly, we stopped moving. The motor was still running but we weren't going anywhere.

Fear clutching my stomach, I cried, "What's the matter?"

"I don't know," Bill said as he quickly threw out the anchor. "It's not the motor and we have plenty of petrol. I'm going over the side to check." Taking off his shirt and trousers, he jumped in. I sat there with Topper, trying not to let him sense my fear. I didn't want him to know that something was wrong. Yet, I didn't want him to think it was normal to take off your clothes and jump overboard.

Bill's head bobbed up. "The propeller came off, but I found it," he said climbing back into the boat, "I'll have it fixed in a minute. I just came to get a new cotter pin. The other one broke," he explained jumping back into the water.

I leaned over the side. When he bobbed to the surface, I called out, "Can I help?"

"No, I'm almost done." Bubbles rose as he went under again. As the minutes ticked by, they seemed to stretch into hours.

Suddenly, the boat jerked. It was Bill. He grinned as he climbed over the side. "She's right, mate," he said, exuding a confidence that I could not match.

"How did you ever find the propeller? It came off quite a way back."

He looked at me and said quietly, almost reverently, "It was a miracle."

By the time we anchored at Redland Bay, it was beginning to mist. We did the unloading, loading procedure and drove on to the school. With relief, Mickey and the girls greeted us. Tables and chairs had been arranged around the school parade ground for a picnic meal. They had eaten dinner with their friends and were anxiously waiting for their costumes.

I helped the girls change just in time for the Grand March. Halfway through the Grand March, the weather turned from misty to windy and wet. We huddled together under shelters, wondering if it would blow over. When it started to rain, we knew there was no hope. People began packing up to go home.

The Ryans, realizing that we had come from the islands, asked if we would like to stay overnight with them. "It will be pretty windy on the bay and it's late," Bernie said. Their offer was an answer to my fervent prayer.

"Thank you," I murmured with relief. Turning to Bill, I smiled weakly. "I think that would be the best thing to do, don't you?" The look on my face pleaded, "I just can't handle another boat ride tonight."

"Yes" he nodded, understanding my plea.

Mickey and Skippy had already made plans to stay with friends. Rusty, not interested in Fancy Dress Balls, was spending the weekend with his fishing buddy, Bob Stockwell.

Bill, Topper and I piled into the car with the girls and followed the Ryans home. It wasn't until we were safely inside the house that my body began to unwind from the afternoon's stress. Happily, the rest of the evening was pure enjoyment. Good friends, light-hearted talk and no rocking boat.

The next morning we said our thank you's and goodbyes, climbed into the car and headed for Redland Bay. When we reached the bay the *Seagull* was not to be found. "It must have drifted," Bill said, bewildered. He got out of the car, walked down to the shore and scanned the beach in both directions. Coming back to the car he mumbled, "I don't see it from here. Let's drive up the road and look."

We did. No boat. We drove down the other way. No boat. "Let's go back to the jetty and ask the man in the kiosk," I suggested.

"Fair enough," Bill said. "I don't think he'll be able to help us, but we can try." He went into the store to ask the owner if knew anything about the boat. In a few minutes, the two of them came out and walked down to the shore. What is this all about? I wondered.

"What's Daddy doing?" Pam wanted to know. Just then the shopkeeper turned to Bill, pointing up with his forefingers; then he pointed down. They spoke for a few more minutes and Bill came back to the car. I knew what he was going to say.

"He told me it's right there," Bill said, waving his arm toward the water. "We should be able to see it at low tide."

A Boat to Float

"You mean the boat sank!" Pam exclaimed, scanning the water for some telltale sign.

"Yes, it did," Dad sighed. "The shopkeeper told me there was a lot of rain and the bay was very rough last night.

"Daddy," Jackie wailed, "how will we get home to Fiddler's Green?"

"The ferry will be here soon," Tia told her. "Don't worry. Dad, do you want us to bring the trolley up to this end of the jetty for you? We can take Topper with us."

"Yes, you girls get the trolley while we unload and park the car."

When they had run off down the jetty, I asked Bill, "Will you be able to save the boat?"

"Well, I'll give it a go," he said. "When we get home I'll call Mr. Jackson. He'll know what to do."

At high tide, Mr. Jackson took Bill and the boys back to Redland Bay. Bill told us what they found. "The tide was still high, but we could see the boat. Mr. Jackson used his boat to push the *Seagull* as close to the beach as he could. When the tide ebbed, water began to pour out of the boat."

I didn't want to interrupt Bill's story, but I did wonder how much water came out through that hole in the side...

Without my asking, Bill said he put a temporary patch on the hole and they bailed the rest of the water by the bucketful. When the boat was light enough to lift, they propped it up so it would float on the morning tide. After they had done all they could, Bill disconnected the electrical parts and they came back to Russell.

At home, Bill put the electrical parts in the oven to dry out. He called Bob's house and told Rusty to meet him in the morning. "I'll be coming on Mr. Jackson's boat when the tide rises," he explained.

When Rusty learned what had happened, he shook his head in disbelief. Then he commented with a grin, "No wonder Bob Stockwell uses a row boat."

Taking the helm, Rusty steered while Mr. Jackson carefully towed the *Seagull* out into deep water and back to the island. At home, Bill flushed the salt water out of the engine, reattached all the electrical parts and reinforced the patch over the hole. I washed the curtains and cushions.

Within days, everything was up and running and ready to go. We were back in business and much wiser for the experience.

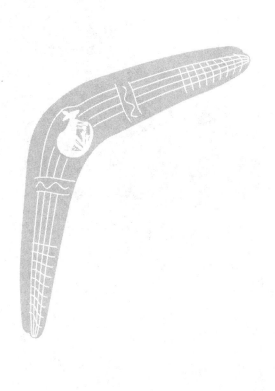

Chapter Eleven

The Essay

I could hear Mickey at his desk, groaning over his homework. I peeked in the door. "What's the matter?"

"Oh, I have to write an essay and I don't know what to write about."

"The jetty?"

"What do you mean, the jetty?"

I sat down on the edge of his bed. "Now that we can come and go with our own boat, I'm realizing how important the jetty is to island living."

"Too right!" Mickey exclaimed, catching hold of the idea. "Let me think." He stared into space a moment, sorting out his facts. "Okay," he said. "How about this? The jetty is our link to the outside world. Its long arm reaches out into the bay to send us off and welcome us when we return home.

More than wood and rails, the jetty has a life of its own. Anyone who comes or goes on the island travels along the jetty. Indeed, the island's livelihood depends upon it. The food on our plates comes about as a result of the jetty."

"Hey, that sounds good," I encouraged.

He smiled and continued, "It runs almost four hundred feet across the mud banks to the bay."

"How did you know that?"

"Mr. Noyes told me. I think he was around when it was built."

"Okay, what else?"

"Well, you already know this. Getting on or off boats is not always easy. At high tide, passengers usually step directly from the boat to the jetty. But with rough seas, it's almost impossible for the boat to get close enough. When it does, because it gyrates wildly, there is danger of passengers slipping down between the boat and the jetty…"

He paused looking at me, remembering an incident. "Mrs. Poynton almost fell in one day. It was scary. Jack grabbed her just in time."

I gently nudged him back to the essay. "Tell me some good things about the jetty."

"Oh, yes! The oysters! The wood posts that support the jetty are underwater most of the time. Because of this, they have an abundance of oysters growing on them. It can't be seen at high tide, but at the end of the jetty there is a cement platform where passengers get off at low tide. This platform is a favorite spot for oyster lovers. All it takes is a sharp knife and a good appetite."

"What else?" I laughed.

"Mmm," he thought for a minute, "the jetty shed?"

The Essay

"Yes, it's an important part of island living."

"Okay. Well..." he mused, "how do I describe it? It's a 12x15 foot storage shed. It juts out at one side of the jetty, twenty feet from the end. It provides shelter from the wind and rain for both people and packages. It has a sliding door on the jetty side and a four-inch ledge around the rest of the building."

"I've heard about that ledge," I said, gazing innocently at the ceiling. Mickey got up and cautiously moved to his desk. I continued, "It seems that while the high-school students are waiting for the morning boat, they amuse themselves by daring each other to walk around the shed on that four-inch ledge. I've been told that their only hand-holds are galvanized nail heads, sticking out on the side of the building. If they slip at high tide, they would become shark meat. At low tide, it's bets on how deeply they would sink into the mud from a twenty-foot drop.

Of course," I challenged, "the Moore boys would never do anything that rash. Would they?"

"Who—us?" Mickey tried to look surprised. "Now, why would we do anything like that?"

"I'm sure you wouldn't," I pretended to agree. But my mother's intuition told me it would take a body cast or crutches to stop boys from toying with danger.

"Should I write about the trolley?" Mickey asked, changing the subject.

"Sure, what would we do without it?"

"Too right." He continued—"A miniature trolley track runs the length of the jetty. It has a flat bottomed car (operated by manpower) that carries heavy loads back and forth. Things like produce, school ports, building supplies, mainland-shopping packages, tired children and sometimes...adults worn out from a day in town."

"Fair dinkum," I smiled, "and the kids love to provide the manpower without always checking to see if anyone is in the way."

"The barge is next," Mickey said.

"Okay, what are you going to write about that?"

"On the opposite side of the shed and near the shore is a cement launching ramp. This is where an old Navy landing barge discharges a truck to pick up farm produce. On Sundays and Wednesdays, the jetty compound bustles with activity. Farmers load stalks of bananas, bags of beans, sacks of potatoes and crates of tomatoes and paw paws. When the last crate is in place, the truck drives back onto the barge. At Redland Bay it will leave the barge and drive to the Farmers Market in Brisbane."

"Don't forget the most important part of barge day," I reminded him.

"What's that?" he frowned, wondering what he had missed.

I laughed. "Barge days are also social events. A time to visit and catch up on island news. Dad says "barge days are better than reading the newspaper."

"He's right," Tia interjected on her way down the hall. "And don't forget the beach," she said over her shoulder.

"I guess she means the shark-proof enclosure for swimmers," Mickey said. "It's okay for the littlies I guess, but not very interesting." I knew what he meant and what he didn't want to say.

Unfortunately, the shark-proof enclosure can't compete with the thrill of diving from the jetty's eight foot-

The Essay

high posts. Even though the older kids realized that sharks were drawn to the shade under the jetty, it didn't discourage them. Shark sightings are too soon forgotten by the young.

"What about fishing from the pier?" Rusty said, joining us. "That's another social event. In the evening we boys go down to the jetty just for the entertainment."

"Too right," Mickey agreed, "I sit beside Butch and listen to him tell stories while he's fishing. That's where I learn about life," he grinned.

"Butch doesn't use a fishing rod," Rusty said, "he winds his fishing line around a coke bottle. You'd be surprised at the number of fish he catches with that thing."

"Butch doesn't get nearly as many as Arthur Milband," Skippy announced, standing in the doorway. "Arthur fishes from the jetty with a net and sometimes a bucket. He lowers a lantern on a rope down to the water so the light will attract the fish. Then he scoops up a whole school of needle-nosed gar in his net or his bucket. The next day, we see him trekking around the island sharing his catch. He has too many fish to eat by himself."

After a moment, Mickey said quietly, "There's something else about the jetty. I'm not going to put it in my essay, but the jetty can be a place of pain. It was on the jetty that three of the bigger kids, egged on by Marvin West, were about to make mincemeat of me. Rusty stepped in and protected me. Later, I had to take Mark Symonds into the jetty shed and warn him to stop picking on my sisters."

"It can be a place of hurt too," Skippy said sadly. "It's where the anti-American bunch influenced others to treat us as trespassers in their country."

"Yeah," Rusty added with a sigh. "And somebody decorated the side of the jetty shed with a big sign. Letters in red paint that read, 'Yankee go home.'"

Mickey, broken-hearted, cried indignantly, "Mom, this is our home! We attend school here! We love our neighbors! We take part in island activities! This is where our friends live. How can one new family cause so much trouble?"

"Yes," I murmured. "The change started at the jetty. It was at the jetty that we understood that some Australians remain kind and true friends—and some do not.

Chapter Twelve

Fun and Games

The day-by-day harassment continued, sometimes funny, sometimes not— but always ridiculous. I decided that the islanders needed to know what was going on. Whether they chose to do anything about it, or not was up to them. Thus began the War of the Bulletin Boards. After one episode I typed a little message and Bill put it up on the bulletin board at the jetty. It said:

> *Congratulations to Susan Symonds and Kay Reed who paraded up and down in front of Fiddler's Green on Saturday morning. Holding their noses, they shouted insults like "Yankee Pig" and "Dirty American." This display gave our visitors a very poor picture of Russell Island girls.*

Or course there were complaints about my using the bulletin board. So I responded with another message:

Fair go for all?

I have heard it said that I should not use the bulletin board for public criticism. Could it be that on this island there are two sets of rules? One group, including Mrs. Runkle and Tom Hamlin, has no problem using the **RKLM News** *to condemn. Other Russell Islanders denounce each other in the* **Sunday Truth.** *Some even use the side of the jetty shed.*

Is it just "Yankees" who are supposed to sit back quietly while their names are blackened by lies and trumped-up charges? In any case, it matters not what we write or where. Some people will believe only what they want. Others, perhaps wiser, will ask, "What is the real truth?"

For weeks, the boys never went out at night without a waddie (that's Australian for a big stick). Mickey's was a beaut. Varnished and polished to a fare-thee-well and ready to use if necessary.

We were never sure how far this situation would be pushed. Copying the Vietnam anti-war demonstrations in the States, a couple of teens who spent a lot of time with Grosse erected a "Yank go home" sign on the jetty hill. It was there to greet me when I returned from a doctor's appointment in Brisbane. I could not believe my eyes. What kind of a person would do a thing like that?

"Did you see the sign!?" Mickey exploded as soon as I walked in the door. "First the jetty shed and now, right where everyone can see it as they come up the hill. What are we going to do?" he moaned.

"First," I said, putting my arm around his shoulders, "we are going to remain calm. These people would like nothing better than to see us all upset and wringing our hands. Second, and this is a job for you, we are going to take a picture of that sign. I'm sure it will come in very handy one day. Would you like to do that for me?"

Given a plan of action he began to relax. "Sure, where's the camera?" I handed him the camera and he went off on his mission.

But it didn't stop there. There was constant tormenting on the school boat. Especially from Grosse. He would flick burnt matchsticks at the boys and call them abusive names. This occurred on three successive trips. Ron was on the boat and witnessed the performance one afternoon. He was appalled at the insults shouted at our children.

Another afternoon, three boys ganged up on Mickey at the jetty after school. But big brother Rusty turned around and ran back to stand with him. After a few thumps from Rusty, the boys left in a hurry, as cowards usually do.

"It sure is good to have a big brother," Mickey told me, when he got home. "Those kids were getting mean."

That night I penned a letter to Mr. Prezzy, the minister of education. It read:

> *I hereby make a formal complaint against an adult being permitted to harass children on the Russell Island to Redland Bay high-school boat. At present, there are twenty-six pupils as well as fare-paying adults being carried on a boat licensed for*

> twenty-nine people. Since the boat proprietor, Mr. Walter Lacey, is finding it difficult to keep order and protect children from aggressive adults, I strongly recommend that the passengers be limited to school children only. Furthermore, Mr. Lacey should be advised of his responsibilities as an adult in sole charge of twenty-six children.

Mr. Prezzy wasn't interested. He let us know that the Russell Island Conveyance Committee had selected Mr. Lacey; they were the ones responsible for his conduct. He advised us that assault, or defamation, was a matter for the police, or a civil action.

My next letter was to Mr. Murphy, the director of education. He suggested that the Conveyance Committee meet to discuss the matter. After the meeting, I wrote back in the formal Australian style:

> Thank you for your prompt attention regarding the high-school ferry boat. A Conveyance Committee meeting was held last night as per your request. At that time a vote of confidence was moved and carried in favor of Mr. Lacey, the boat proprietor.
>
> In conjunction with this, I have been asked by some of the parents to place before you the findings of the meeting. They would like me to explain that their vote was given since only a few weeks remain of the school year. Points brought forth in the meeting causing the most concern were as follows:

Fun and Games

1. *Petrol fumes in the boat have made several children ill;*
2. *A child is reported to have broken a rope on the life-saving gear;*
3. *The new, larger boat promised by Mr. Lacey to be in service by mid-year has not been realized.*

My original complaint to your office pales beside the vastly more serious problem of jeopardizing the lives and health of the children. It has been brought to light that at least four sets of parents have cautioned their children against sitting in the boat's cabin. These children have complained of nausea from inhaling petrol fumes. The outside deck area seats from six to eight children, almost a third of the total passenger capacity. Naturally, when a child must choose between illness and being jammed into a third of the allotted area, one can expect discipline problems.

The broken rope is even more frightening. As I understand it, these ropes are attached to floats. In the event of the boat sinking, the children should be able to hang onto them while awaiting rescue. If these ropes can be broken by "horseplay," how reliable would they be in heavy seas with several children clinging to them?

Since the end of the school year is close and the new larger boat has been promised again, some parents would like to settle back with their fingers crossed to wait out the remainder of the year.

Personally, and particularly with the typhoon season approaching, I continue to be alarmed for the health and safety of the children. I must go on record as one of those who could not vote with confidence for Mr. Lacey. It is requested that you keep this letter on file for future reference. Thank you for your prompt attention.

Marvin West continued to stir up the other boys against Rusty and Mickey. Rusty came home each night upset and frustrated. "He was at it again today," he cried out as he entered the door. "Pushing and shoving and daring me to fight him."

I tried to be calm. I reminded him that he had been taught to turn the other cheek and to live by the Golden Rule. "It was all right to protect your brother," I explained, "but it's another matter to fight for our own satisfaction."

That evening, during our walk-talk time I put my arm around Bill's shoulder. "Would you mind going down to Ron and Jack's? I want to talk to them about this situation with Rusty and Marvin."

"That's a good idea," he said. "I don't want to encourage fighting but something has to be done. Since it was Ron who witnessed the harassment on the boat, he would have a good picture of what's going on."

Ron and Jack warmly welcomed us, as they always do. Over a cup of tea I brought up the subject of Rusty and Marvin. "What would an Australian do in such a case?" I asked.

Jack, who had witnessed a lot of street life in Sydney, leaned forward in his chair and said seriously, "There is only one way to stop a bully. You have to fight him."

"But we've always taught our kids not to fight others."

"That is a good rule," Ron, the retired minister, agreed, "but there are times when action is necessary."

I looked at Bill. "Rusty wouldn't have a problem with that, would he?"

"Rusty can handle anyone," he said with a father's pride.

We finished our tea, thanked Ron and Jack and headed for home. "I'll let you take care of this," I told Bill with a sigh of relief. He put his arm around me. We walked home, feeling as though a heavy load had been lifted from our shoulders.

In the morning, Bill told Rusty he had permission to fight Marvin the next time Marvin invited him to. "That's if I can catch him," Rusty grinned. When he came home from school that afternoon, he told us he was going to fight Marvin the next day after school.

Bill went down to the jetty early to be on hand, but stayed up on the hill out of sight. Just before the boat docked, Rusty went into the WC (Australian for water closet, or toilet) and changed into his sports uniform. "So I wouldn't ruin my good school clothes," he explained later. All the children on the boat understood he had taken Marvin up on his dare.

As soon as the boat docked, Marvin was the first one off. He ran up the hill with Rusty in swift pursuit. When Rusty finally caught him and demanded that he fight it out, Marvin signaled three other boys to help him.

That's when Bill stepped out of the shadows. "You kids stay out of it," he said quietly. His voice and manner froze them in their tracks. "This fight is between Rusty and Marvin and it's going to stay that way."

Marvin, after all his brash talk and days of shoving Rusty around, turned out to be an absolute ninny. Rusty thrashed him soundly before he allowed him to run off home.

There were no more taunts from that quarter. But Leo Grosse was still to be dealt with. The fun and games were not over.

Chapter Thirteen

Will It Ever End?

Every day, when Bill went down for the mail, Grosse stood on his porch waving a waddie and shouting obscenities. "He was over on Routledge's tank stand today, yelling his head off," Bill reported handing me the mail. "You wouldn't believe what he said. During all my years as a sailor, I never heard anything that bad."

"Something has got to be done about this," I said, trying to think.

"Well, you can't arrest a person just for talking," Bill grumbled as he unloaded the tucker bag.

Sifting through the possibilities, I paused. "Too bad we can't tape him, but the tape recorder isn't working."

"Proper dingo," Bill said, disappointed.

"I know what to do!" I exclaimed. Another bright idea had just been born.

"You can still use the tape recorder. He doesn't know it's broken. Just hold it up when he starts yelling and he'll think you really are taping him!"

"Fair dinkum," Bill smiled.

The next day, he settled the recorder strap over his shoulder and went off down the road. Grosse was in his usual place waiting for him to pass. As soon as he started shouting, Bill held the tape recorder up so it could be plainly seen. When Grosse realized what Bill was holding, he stopped mid-sentence.

"There was not another word from him," Bill grinned, reporting the event. "I continued down the road in peace and quiet. There was no sign of him on the way back, either. I think it worked," he said, "but you never know what that type will come up with next."

A week later, Bill came home, holding up a letter. "It's from Grosse," he announced.

"Really? What is it?"

"Here." With a funny look on his face, he passed it to me.

I scanned the letter. "Why, Jack Wynn sent this same type of form letter when he wanted us to pay for his fence. Now we know where he got the idea. Well, I'll answer it the same way I answered Jack." I wrote:

> *After your verbal notice in January requesting that we contribute to a new divisional fence, we inspected the existing fence between our two properties. At that time we found a majority of the posts well seated and firm with one strand of barbed wire. Since ours is a small-crop farm, it would not be sound business to finance a stock-proof fence. We propose and agree to the following:*

1. *Replacement of defective and missing posts.*
2. *Repair and replacement of broken or missing barbed wire.*
3. *The addition of two strands of plain wire, which would constitute a sufficient divisional fence."*

Grosse responded by borrowing a bulldozer and proceeding to destroy our fence. When Bill went up into the field to check on the commotion, Grosse deliberately tried to run him down with the dozer. After demolishing the fence, he replaced it with a stock-proof fence. We thought that was the end of the matter until, months later, we received a letter from his lawyer. It demanded payment for the fence.

"What a colossal nerve!" I fumed.

"This time, we'll answer through his lawyer," Bill said quietly.

"Jolly good," I declared. "Let's see…what was the fence worth that he bulldozed?" We listed damages trying to be very fair and sent it off to his lawyer.

To: McCafferty and Waters
Re: Leo Grosse—Payment of dividing fence
As a convenience to ourselves and to your client, we would be willing to deduct our share of the fence cost (which is $47.50) from the total due us. Following is the bill for your client:
Destroying our boundary fence without prior permission or notification.

(ref: photographs and police report)	*$20.50*
Crops lost carrying out the above	*$44.75*

Drainage ditch destroyed causing erosion $15.35
Total damage $80.60
Minus our cost of the dividing fence.
Balance due us $33.10

This amount is due and must be paid within seven (7) days from the date hereof, otherwise we intend to seek instructions as to the institution of further proper proceedings.

This foolishness went on and on between courts and solicitors. Finally, Bill wrote one last letter:

Judge - Magistrates Court
Dear Sir,

On 9 March, 1967 I received a notice from solicitors on behalf of L. Grosse, stating specifications for a four-strand barbed wire fence. No reply to our offer was received from Mr. Grosse who, without notification, hired a bulldozer and demolished the existing fence.

No further communication was made until eleven months later, when we received a court summons initiated by Mr. Grosse. Our solicitor negotiated with Mr. Grosse's solicitor for three months. Finally, feeling that the situation had become ridiculous I indicated to my solicitor that a court hearing would be preferable. Whereupon Mr. Grosse quickly settled and the fence was erected.

My wife and I, who own the farm jointly, have just received bills for court costs. I must apologize for not understanding the laws in your country, laws that say a man can destroy his neighbor's fence and force him to pay for rebuilding it. However, after twenty years with the American Navy (four years served in Naval Intelligence) I understand the necessity of enforcing laws.

Since I do not feel that the court costs are an honest bill incurred by myself, I would prefer to serve the jail sentence instead. Therefore, I duly request of the court that I be permitted to serve my wife's term of imprisonment also. For her to leave our seven children uncared for would cause untold hardship.

Respectfully yours,
William R. Moore

For some reason the court never replied. We heard no more about fences, solicitors or judges. Unfortunately, this was not the end of the Grosse story. He continued harassing and attempting to get Bill to fight him at every turn. Remembering Ron and Jack's sage advice, it seemed the only solution to the bullying tactics was to meet him on his own turf. I wrote another notice for the jetty bulletin board:

NOTICE

WHEREAS Leo Grosse parked his truck outside my house at night and, with two other islanders, threw rocks on my roof;
AND WHEREAS he has falsely accused me of assaulting him with a chain;
AND WHEREAS he has for the past two years constantly sought to ruin my name and reputation;
AND WHEREAS he has maligned and insulted my wife, my children and my country;

I hereby state publicly that if he wishes to carry out his threat of bodily harm to my person, I will make myself available at the main jetty compound on the 8th of August.

When the appointed day arrived, Grosse was nowhere to be found. "He went to the mainland on the early boat," Chris Wilson told Bill. Undaunted, Bill made himself available at the jetty when the late afternoon boat was due.

An unusual number of people were already at the jetty in anticipation of a good scrap. They had heard Grosse's threats and wanted to see if he would stick to his word. Just before the boat docked, Tom Hamlin arrived at the jetty compound. He eased his car next to the jetty and backed it up facing the road.

When the boat docked, Grosse climbed off, carrying a heavy stick. He brandished it at Bill, shouting empty threats. Swiftly he climbed into Tom's waiting car and was whisked out of Bill's reach. I'm sure the memory of Marvin's recent thrashing by Rusty was the reason for his desperate escape.

Those anticipating a good fight wandered off disappointed. At home, Bill cautioned, "Don't think this is the end of Grosse, he'll find someone else to hide behind. That kind always do."

Bill was right, it didn't take him long. Becoming more cowardly, Grosse incited the high-school students to abuse our younger children on the school boat. Again, I responded via the bulletin board:

NOTICE

A city, town or island is often no better than its inhabitants. If our island is aiming at mediocrity, it can boast of the help of Amy Rowlings, Susan Symonds and Lucy Porter.

On Thursday, both Susan and Amy deliberately tripped Pamela Moore as she walked along the isle of the MV Titan on her way to the WC and again on the way back. When Pam started to cry, Amy showed her fine upbringing in a profuse, but not sincere, apology.

We're not really surprised that Russell Island high schoolers amuse themselves by tormenting a seven-year-old. It follows a pattern that has been going on for over a year.

One particular incident we remember well, from the bruises on Jackie's foot. She was just six years old when Marvin West slammed his heavy port down on her feet.

Special mention must go to Susan Symonds for her part in making the island a bit lower. Congratulations on the cute way you thumb your nose and wiggle your rear at Mr. Moore when he passes by. We must also mention the harassing tactics of Amy and Lucy, who jumped in front of the Moore's car as Rusty drove home after school.

A note of caution: While an "accident" may provide the island with gossip and recriminations, it could also land someone in the hospital. It would be safer to stick to your previous tactics of throwing sticks at the boys and hitting them when they can't hit back.

That evening Bill and I reviewed the situation, walking under the stars. Bill summed it up. "We've notified the school board without any results. Grosse isn't going to change. The parents are not interested in controlling their children. The police can't do anything—although they would like to. At this point, our only solution is to send the children to school on Jack Noyes' boat." He paused, "I think I'll go to Brisbane tomorrow."

"What for?"

"Oh, there are some things I need to take care of."

Bill had decided to go to the top. He went to Brisbane and had a chat with the Minister for Justice and Attorney-General. Sympathetic and understanding, Mr. Aikens later sent us a copy of a letter he had written to the Minister for Works and Housing in Brisbane.

Dear Mr. Hodges,

Mr. William Raymond Moore of Russell Island, an American ex-Patriot, interviewed me recently with a complaint of the law and order state of affairs on the Island. He states that over a period of years he has been plagued by three or four neighbors led by one Leo Grosse, who threw stones on his roof and threatened to run down his dog and his children by motor cars.

I should be obliged if you would have this matter investigated with a view to alleviation.

Yours faithfully,

The problem was investigated and things began to level out. "Someone from Brisbane with a heavy hand of authority must have had a chat with Grosse," Bill said one day. "He certainly has quieted down."

"What a relief," I murmured. "Having a new head teacher seems to be helping, too. Mr. Fitzpatrick is more interested in encouraging unity for the benefit of the children than promoting anti-Americanism. Now, perhaps Fiddler's Green can return to normal."

"What is normal?" Bill asked. "It's been so long, I've forgotten."

I laughed. "Well, if I tried to define it for you today, I'd probably have to change the definition tomorrow."

I was right. A letter we received from America gave "normal" a whole new meaning.

Chapter Fourteen

Aunt Jac

As soon as Bill walked in with the mail, I knew something was wrong. "Read this," he said, holding out an airmail letter. "It's from my cousin Christine." The news was not good. Aunt Jac had gone to a neighbor's house on an errand. When she returned, Uncle Guy's bed was ablaze. She was able to put the fire out and get help, but Uncle Guy survived only a few days.

"Oh, no!" Stunned, I sank into a chair. We were both silent as I sat there remembering. Some time ago, Aunt Jac had written that after Uncle Guy passed his ninetieth birthday, it was difficult for him to keep warm. "He sleeps close to the wood stove," she wrote, "and often opens the stove door for extra warmth."

I was finally able to speak. "Perhaps a spark from the stove landed on his bed.

Thank God Aunt Jac wasn't asleep when it happened. The whole house would have gone up in flames."

"I wonder what she'll do now," Bill said slowly. "She's over eighty and shouldn't be there by herself using a wood stove and kerosene lamps."

Forty years earlier, Uncle Guy had been a theater manager and Aunt Jac an actress. Their careers had taken them across America and, later, across the ocean to perform in England. When it was time to retire, they returned to the family country property in Morrill, Maine. There, among the woods, they made friends with the birds and animals. They developed a knowledge of the land and a passion for growing things the natural way. Many years passed as they enjoyed the simple life.

I first met Aunt Jac when we were stationed in Brunswick, Maine. I was twenty-seven and she was a petite seventy-year-old. She had so much energy she wore me out. During the afternoon visit, we walked all over the property. She introduced me to her orchard, her gardens and her pine forest. Aunt Jac took an interest in our children and often sent them books, pictures and little things that children love. Our last visit was in 1957 just before we left for Japan. We had kept in touch ever since.

My face brightened. "Hon, I just thought of something."

Bill looked at me, wary of the key words, "Hon" and "thought" used in the same sentence. He knew it would probably involve a lot of effort on his part. He didn't say anything but waited patiently, his eyebrows slightly raised in a question mark.

"You know, we've always wanted a grandmother for the children, but we've lived so far away. And now, with my mother gone and your mother so ill, it will never happen. What if...?" I glanced at him to see if I should continue.

"You want to ask Aunt Jac to come live with us?"

"Yes! What do you think?"

"Well... we could ask. But we probably should wait until she copes with the shock of Uncle Guy's death."

"Jolly good, I'll wait a few weeks. Since it takes a letter three weeks to get there, she'll be over the first shock and perhaps wondering what to do next."

In writing the letter, I mentioned that we would love to have her come to live with us in Australia. "Don't worry about deciding right off," I wrote, "take as much time as you need to make the decision."

In a few weeks we received a letter from Bill's cousin Jackie, thanking us for offering to have Aunt Jac. She had been very concerned because her husband's job made it impossible for them to take care of her. To reassure Jackie, I wrote at length about Australia in general and our life on Russell Island.

Dear Jackie,

Thank you for your letter. We were delighted that our plan to have Aunt Jac didn't sound too impossible for you to consider.

Australia is a warm, friendly continent tucked away at the end of the world, isolated from most of the world's cavorting. This seclusion bothered me at first. I knew that somewhere out there life was teeming with action and I had very little knowledge of what was going on. Gradually, I learned to appreciate the peacefulness of not having to worry about the rest of the world.

Everything here in Australia is very much like the US may have been ten, twenty or fifty years ago—depending on where you live. In our household shipment, we found some 1963 Newsweek magazines from Rusty's seventh-grade class. Five years later, they are still topical reading over here. Either the world hasn't changed, or we just haven't found out about it yet. Except, of course, the major issues—wars and elections.

The Aussies' best trait—and worst vice—is their friendly, relaxed manner. Their favorite expression is, "She's right, mate!" meaning, it will pass for now. Americans and Japanese are doing much of the building and developing of this country's resources. The Australians often complain about it, but do nothing to change the situation.

The different states, being so large, vary a great deal. New South Wales and Victoria are probably the most advanced and Queensland the farthest behind. We seldom hear anything about Tasmania, the island to the south, and very little about the large city of Perth in Western Australia—although it's supposed to be progressing rapidly.

Our Russell Island is nestled in Redland Bay, between Queensland's coast and Stradbroke's protective North Island. Except for the climate, Russell Island is very much like rural Maine... dusty roads, shady woods and open fields. Aunt Jac may get homesick for the beautiful white snow scenes, or the thrill of spring's arrival, but not having to cope with the rigors of winter will be some compensation.

Aunt Jac

During the summer, there are a few very hot days, just as in any climate. Our March is like your August: humid and sticky. The winter months are lovely, cool, crisp, light-jacket weather.

There are many people on Russell close to Aunt Jac's age, who are keen on gardening and enjoy cooking special dishes. She'll love the way plants grow in this climate and will be able to indulge herself in gardens and flower beds. Three strong boys will be on hand to do the digging.

We've always wanted a grandmother. Someone to sew on a button, listen to a sad tale and teach little girls to be young ladies. That brings us to the difficult part. As much as she loves children, will Aunt Jac be happy living with seven of them? I'm sure it won't be an easy adjustment. Six of the children go to school on the mainland and are away all day. Weekdays are reasonably quiet, but weekends and summer vacations are quite different.

We will be able to give Aunt Jac the rural life she is used to, in a much softer climate. She'll have many acquaintances her own age. During the years, we have adopted several grandmothers, but it's not the same as being family. Aunt Jac would be a link to our American heritage and family background.

If you need any additional information, or if we can help in any other way, please let us know.
Love and Blessings

That afternoon, as we worked on making blocks for a septic tank, I told Bill about the letter. "I reckon there's nothing else we can do. We'll just have to wait and see what happens."

"Well," Bill responded, shoveling gravel into a bucket, "we can move along with the block work while we're waiting. We've just about enough blocks to start building the tank. Rusty has the pit almost finished. He's doing a great job with the digging. That area is all hard clay. When the septic tank is finished, we can put a flush toilet in under the house."

"In that case," I said, dumping a bucket of gravel into the cement mixer, "thank God for our electric mixer and the power to run it! We'll get plenty of use out of it if we go ahead with plans to make a room for Aunt Jac."

"Too right," Bill said pausing to leaning on his shovel, "it looks like it's going to be another big job, though."

"Show me what you plan to do," I said, wiping my dusty hands across my work pants.

"Okay. It's time for a break, anyway." He took my hand and we walked under the house past the laundry area. "I want to build the room on this side of the house, so we can put in windows for plenty of light. Aunt Jac likes morning sunshine. It will face north to keep it cool in the summer. To make it big enough, we'll have to dig back into the hill three feet and put in a retaining wall. Then we'll pour a cement floor. I'll extend the floor to the whole area under the house.

"Jolly good! That means I'll have a cement floor in the laundry area too!"

"Yes, and we'll have the foundation for a storage room and game area. By the time we're finished pouring the floor, we should be able to afford a ping-pong table for the game room."

"Wonderful," I applauded. "How big will Aunt Jac's room be?"

"I'm thinking 10x12 feet."

"Sounds like a good plan, but we're not even sure she's coming yet. Although she did say she's considering the idea. In the meantime, I think I'll write tonight to see how she is getting along."

"Jolly good, it would help if we knew when—or if—she's coming."

That evening, after entertaining the littlies with the ritual two chapters from *The Adventures of the Famous Five*, I settled down at my typewriter:

Dear Aunt Jac,

We are delighted that you are considering our invitation to come to Australia. I really think you will like it. The climate will be the biggest change, but there are so many new plants to grow and foods to sample, I don't think you'll have a chance to get homesick.

Over here, it's possible to keep flowers and vegetables growing all year round. Many of the islanders are keen gardeners. The Horticultural Society is flourishing and hosts two well-attended flower shows each year.

We have a Country Women's Association that is somewhat like your Grange. Our island branch meets once a month. They sponsor a library of over a thousand books. We also have a Country Extension Library in Brisbane that will send you a selection of books monthly—or weekly. The children get all of their books from there. The library mails them over and we mail them back at no cost.

Fiddler's Green is right on the main road, five minutes from the post office and fifteen minutes from the jetty. Just down the hill in the other direction is Miss Watts' farm. She grows everything imaginable and loves the Organic Gardening *books you send. I'm sure the two of you will get along famously.*

We think of you often and look forward to hearing of your plans.

Love and Blessings

Chapter Fifteen

Will She or Won't She?

We sent the letter off and started counting the days. "It will be three weeks before she gets the letter," I told Bill, "and another three weeks before we get an answer."

"Mmm," he said, "and she might not answer right away. That..." he paused to do a quick calculation, "is about two months."

"Well, if that's the case, we probably shouldn't mention Aunt Jac to the kids unless they ask. There is enough anticipation as it is."

"If you consider the septic tank a cause for anticipation, you're right. The girls and Topper want to use it as a swimming pool while the cement is curing. I told them it would be okay."

It wasn't long before their dreams of a swimming pool came true. The septic tank was eight feet long, four feet wide and six feet deep. When Bill started pumping in water from the well, the kids gathered around to watch it rise. Bill stopped at the four-foot level. Tia looked up in dismay. "I can jump in, but I won't be able to climb out."

"I've got that all under control," her dad told her, "I'll fix a little ladder for you so you can get out. Just don't ever go in there without telling your mom or me."

"We won't," they promised.

"And be sure to watch out for Topper."

"We will," they promised.

It was great fun while it lasted. Even the big boys enjoyed taking a dip to cool off after working in the fields. The septic tank inspired renewed interest in the "real" swimming pool. One night at dinner, Rusty asked, "Dad, when are we going to build a real swimming pool?"

Bill looked up from cutting Topper's meat. "It will be a while yet, we still have a lot of blocks to make." "Blocks" was the trigger word.

"Aunt Jac!" Mickey said, jumping in where angels—and Mom—didn't want him to tread. "When's she coming?" he asked the key question.

I sighed, bracing myself for the inevitable deluge of advice and suggestions. "We don't know yet if she plans to come, but she says she's thinking about it. To help her decide, I sent letter to tell her all about the island."

"Did you tell her about all the birds?" Jackie asked.

Before I could answer, Mickey said, "Yeah, you should tell her how they follow the tractor looking for grubs when we plow."

"I'd tell her about the way the Curlew wails at night," Tia added. "Sounds just like a person crying. It's scary."

"Well, what about the racket kookaburras make in the morning?" Pam asked. "They wake me up every day with their ha, ha, ha's."

"What about the magpies?" Topper interrupted.

"Righto," Rusty agreed, "they come right up to the porch railing and eat out of Jackie's hand. Aunt Jac would like those. And," he looked at Topper, "what about the pee wees that travel with them? They look just like pint-sized magpies."

"Maybe she'll think they are baby magpies," Topper beamed, laughing at his own wit.

"She'll like the butcher bird," Skippy threw in, "and the flocks of pelicans sailing high in the sky."

"Don't forget the bluies and greenies." We were back to Jackie. "Tell her they're bigger than a parakeet, but smaller than a parrot. I like them best because they're so pretty."

Since we were on a roll that wasn't going to stop right away, I added my bit. "I like the little swallows that nest around the house. Only God could design something that tiny. My favorite, though, is the bee eater. I love the way it trills, but I don't like it when it eats bees. What do you think, Dad?"

"My favorite are the hawks. We have quite a few species here. They are sooo graceful the way they soar," he emphasized, waving his hands above his head.

Skippy couldn't resist a little drama. "Shouldn't you tell her about the blue-tongue lizard and the frilly lizard, the spiny ant eater, the bandicoot, the wallabies and..." he paused dramatically, "the snakes?"

"Well, Skip, I guess we'll have to save those for later." No telling where that trail would lead us and it was getting late. "If everyone's finished, we'll say prayers and you can get your chores done. Dad and I are going for a walk."

The walk wasn't quite that quick. Topper had to be readied for bed, the girls' baths needed to be supervised and finally… story time. I read two more chapters of *The Adventures of the Famous Five*. The boys finished the dishes and settled down with their homework. We were free.

Outside, we inhaled deep breaths of the fresh night air. "Ahh," I breathed, "I bet most people in the States don't know what fresh clean air is really like."

"Probably not, judging from what we hear about their pollution problems," Bill said, looking up to check the sky for tomorrow's weather. "It's going to be a good day; we'll be able to make some more blocks."

Walking silently for a while, we listened to the different sounds of generator motors. We could always tell who was at home by the noise of their generator. Each motor had a unique sound. Since electric power had come to the island, a lot of the generators were now silent.

Finally, unwound and refreshed we began to chat. "The children are excited about Aunt Jac," I said wistfully. "If she decides to come it will be a gigantic undertaking for her—and for us, but well worth it."

"It would be good for them to have a grandmother and Aunt Jac shouldn't be alone," Bill agreed. "Perhaps we'll get a letter soon."

He was right. Aunt Jac wrote that she had made the decision to come, but she was concerned that she might not fit in. I replied:

Dear Aunt Jac,
It was with a big hurrah and sigh of relief that we received your letter. As the Australians say, "You're

one of our mob." It's a tremendous undertaking to move after living in one house for a long time. To leave friends and country is something that takes special gumption. A year is a long wait, but it will give us time to work out nice accommodations for you.

As for pulling your own weight, I don't think you need worry about that. In a family of nine, living on a farm, there is something to do for every age, inclination or talent. If you want to sew there's sewing, if you want to read there are piles of books everywhere. If you want to plow a field we usually have one that needs it. Bake a cake, write a letter, take a walk, they all fit in with something that needs doing.

If you're set in your ways, please let us know what they are so we can work around them. It will be much easier than your trying to adapt to nine of us. Change is our middle name. We've done a lot of it over the years—especially trying to get this place established.

Bill says financially you are very well set for life on the island. Medical care is free. You will certainly have enough money for outings, special foods, books, etc. An Australian pensioner gets about $50.00 per month to live on. The US Embassy told Bill that if he is your sponsor, you will not need a sum of money to enter the country.

I hope I've answered all your questions. Ask as many as you like. The children are excited at the prospect of having a "grandmother" after all these years.

Love and Blessings

At dinner time, I broke the news to the children. "We got a letter from Aunt Jac today. She says she will come." I paused, waiting for the din to subside. "But it will take her about a year to get everything in order." I paused again while they all moaned. "We have to remember that it requires a lot of time to get ready to move. Didn't it take us quite a while?"

"Fair dinkum," Rusty said, "we worked on it for a whole year."

"I remember making the scrap books," Tia piped up.

"We did have a lot of fun doing those, didn't we?" I smiled. "They helped us to fit in when we got here because we already knew a lot about Australia. Aunt Jac is a bit worried about fitting in. I told her she would find a lot of familiar things right here in our house. The gold and white prints on the folding screen came from Aunt Jac."

"And the *Reader's Digest* books," Skippy said. "I like the stories in those."

"Mom, remember the calendar pictures we framed to decorate the sun porch? Aunt Jac gave us that calendar."

"Righto Pam, those are beautiful pictures of Hummel figurines. They do look nice on the wall, don't they?" She agreed with a nod and a grin.

"What about all the garden magazines?" Bill spoke up, "and the books on farming that she sent? They've been a lot of help."

"Mom, remember those cloth prints of Mickey Mouse that she gave us when we were little?" Mickey said reminiscing. "You sewed them on our pajamas that year. I still have mine in my drawer."

"She sent us the baby Jesus in the manger to set up

when we do Christmas things," Jackie said, thinking about what was coming up.

"Christmastime!" Topper clapped his hands. He was a little early but we appreciated the thought.

On that note, I decided it was time for after-dinner prayer. The boys needed to get their homework started, but no one could leave the table until the thanksgiving prayer was said. Prayer after meals was a family tradition that served a double purpose. Picky eaters were apt to eat more while they waited and slow pokes, not wanting to be left behind, made sure they finished on time. And all of us learned to express thanks. Well-used traditions tend to smooth the bumps of living.

"The Playhouse"

Chapter Sixteen

Things to Make

With the lack of rain, planting was practically at a standstill. While the other farmers were taking time to relax, we spent more time making the large blocks and smaller bricks. We decided that a nice touch for the outside wall of Aunt Jac's room would be yellow ocher split-blocks to match the gold trim of the house. While they were drying, we worked on the next project.

We had already made enough brick-sized blocks for our WC. Bill marked out the wall for this toilet area and began to lay the bricks. When I went downstairs to announce lunch time, he had half of one wall done. I stood there—as I always do—to check the job. That's important with Bill, because sometimes he gets carried away with a project. He feels that finishing the job is more important than how it looks. Reason number two is—I'm the one who reads the instructions.

"Hon, aren't there supposed to be grooves between the bricks in a brick wall?"

"What do you mean?"

"Well, I was reading the directions and they say to lay a bed of mortar along several bricks, then you 'butter' both ends of a brick with mortar and press it down in place. After you lay a few bricks, you use a jointer tool to smooth the mortar between the bricks."

"Oh, well, this is all right, isn't it? I'm just spreading the mortar out on the bricks."

"Well, it's all right if you are going to render the whole wall later. Are you?"

"No, this will do," he shrugged.

"Let's go have lunch," I said, closing the discussion.

Upstairs, we talked about what still needed to be done. "What's the next step?" I asked innocently.

"Well, when the WC is bricked in, I'll start digging into the hill to enlarge the area for Aunt Jac's room. We have a lot of dirt to be moved."

"Perhaps I could do the brickwork while you dig," I offered.

"Those bricks are pretty heavy," he warned.

"I can do it," I assured him.

That afternoon began my apprenticeship toward becoming a master bricklayer. It was not easy. Those 4x8-inch blocks were solid. Much larger than a standard-sized brick, they weighed at least five pounds each. As the wall grew taller, I had to lift them higher. Selecting the next brick, I mumbled to myself, "This is not my idea of a career."

"Place a bed of mortar, butter the brick ends, smooth the mortar with the jointer tool..." I reminded myself, as I fitted each block into place. It took almost a week to get the job done. But it was worth it when I stood back and triumphantly surveyed the finished project. I didn't say anything to Bill, because the contrast between my walls and the one he started was statement enough. *I wonder if this qualifies me to be a master builder, I mused.* With the walls finished, Bill installed the flush and filled the septic tank. We finally had "proper" plumbing!

While I was building the brick walls, the boys had helped with the excavation into the hill. Bill poured a three-foot retaining wall and when it was set, he began to finish the wall with bricks. Since this wall would be covered with paneling, I happily retired from my bricklaying job. I had made my point and it was time to get ready for Christmas.

We gathered our Pack-O-Fun magazines Aunt Jac had sent from the States. The children poured through them looking for just the right Christmas gifts to make. "Mom," Tia asked, "what's a Styrofoam tray? I need two for my project."

Oh dear, how do you explain a Styrofoam tray? "Those are sort of plastic trays they sell meat in at the grocery stores in the States," I said. "I've never seen them in Australia."

"They don't have plastic jugs here, either," Skippy warned. "So don't plan on using any of those."

We spent hours in the sunroom with pots of glue, colored paper, toilet paper rolls, pretty buttons and bits of lace. We made Christmas cards with wax paper etchings, macaroni puppets, doll house furniture and tree decorations.

Jackie and Pam wanted wigs of long black hair. I spent hours sewing strands of black yarn onto the tops of old silk stockings.

Skippy made a hammock for the girls. He sewed two burlap bags together and attached wooden strips to each end. The baling twine and long needle we used to secure the tops of potato bags for market came in handy for that project.

Bill helped Mickey and Rusty make scooters for the girls using old roller skates. "They've done a great job," he said proudly. "They look like the scooters we had when we were little."

"It's too bad we don't have pavement for them to run on," I remarked.

"I know," Bill sighed. "They won't last long, but the boys are having a lot of fun making them. This afternoon they'll be out in the shed painting the scooters red, so don't let the girls go out there." I assured him I would keep the girls busy.

A few days later, Mickey made a strange request. "Can I have the privy?" he asked. "We're not using it any more."

"No, we're not, but what on earth are you going to do with a privy?"

"Well, I thought I'd move it over into the orchard and make a play house for the girls."

"Hey, that sounds like a good idea, but the seats would have to be taken out. And, it would have to be thoroughly cleaned and painted."

"I know," he said, "I've got it all worked out. I want to make a cement floor first. Then I'm going to make an upstairs."

"How are you going to do that?" I wondered.

"Daddy said he would show me what to do."

Things to Make

"How will the girls get up there?"

"I'll make a ladder on the wall," he explained patiently.

"I can put a window in downstairs," Rusty offered.

"I'll help too," Skippy joined in.

The girls and Topper were warned by a few stern words from big brother Rusty to keep away from the project. They knew something was going on, but could only wonder—what?

Between them, the boys loaded the five-foot-square, nine-foot-tall privy onto the tractor trailer. They towed it to the new cement floor in the orchard. Mickey made a very clever loft with a door that opened outside for a great view. After Rusty put in a window, they painted inside and out with leftover cream-colored house paint and trimmed it with burnt orange.

Skippy put a fresh coat of paint on the little table and chair set that had been in the family since the boys were tiny tots. I sewed orange gingham curtains for the window and Bill put up a miniature clothes line. The privy was now a beautiful, clean, two-story playhouse.

After all the gifts were open Christmas morning, Mickey stood up and said with mock seriousness, "Oh, we forgot something, but I can't remember what."

He didn't catch the girls or Topper asleep. They all shouted, "The privy!"

"Oh, yes!" Rusty snapped his fingers, hiding a grin. "We were going to do something with that, but I don't remember what."

The girls were beginning to look worried. Topper shouted, "You did! I saw you." No one was going to fool him.

"Maybe we could go look at it," Skippy suggested, stepping back quickly before the girls knocked him over on the way out. We could hear the squeals of pleasure as Mickey ushered them in. They climbed the ladder to the loft and flung open the door. "Thank you, boys!" they shouted loud enough for the whole island to hear.

They were thrilled. From the loft, they could keep an eye on all the farm activities. They spent hours doing "laundry" in a bucket of water to hang on the line. They fixed meals in the house kitchen to eat at "Little Fiddler's Green."

The hammock was hung between two nearby trees. The girls paraded around in their new long black hair. At nap time, they tried to rock Topper asleep in the hammock. Sometimes, they succeeded.

Bill congratulated the boys on their project. "Mickey, that was a great idea; you have all done a wonderful job working together. I'm surprised you were able to finish on time with all the farm work to do, and Rusty's exams."

In the midst of all the bustle, Rusty had "sat" for his Senior pass. Australians use the term "sit for exams" because that's what the students do. They sit for hours writing page after page. No multiple choice questions here. Rusty churned out six written exam papers, two each week for three weeks, the equivalent of six term papers. We wouldn't know the results until after the Christmas holidays but were sure he had done well. He always did, even though he moaned that he probably wouldn't make it.

The good news arrived in January. Rusty had passed with flying colors! He began to think of going to college in the States. The Fergusons, old friends we had met in Japan, wrote from Yakima, Washington. "Would Rusty like to stay with us and go to college over here?" For years they had talked about it in their letters and now it was time to make a decision. Washington seemed so far away, but I could understand Rusty wanting to go.

Bill came home from a trip to Brisbane with some encouraging news. "I've found out that if you're an American and want to go back to the States, you can work your way back on a freighter. Would you like to do that?" he asked, looking at Rusty.

"Yes," Rusty said quietly. But inside I knew he was jumping up and down with excitement.

"You'll have to put in an application and wait until they have an opening," Bill explained. "We don't know how long that will take. Have you thought of what you want to do in the meantime?"

"I think I can get a job on a farm on the mainland. I'll go see tomorrow."

He had no trouble getting a job. There was always a need for farmhands at Redland Bay. After a few weeks of working on a tomato farm, he came home one night with an announcement.

"I've made a great discovery," he said.

"Fair dinkum," his dad was impressed.

"I know one thing I don't want to do with the rest of my life."

"What's that?" I leaped for the bait, like a fish to a worm.

"Farming," he said with a straight face.

We all laughed at something that wasn't really a joke.

Chapter Seventeen

A Son Is Grown

It's getting a little cooler," Bill said as we settled into the gazebo, holding our Sunday morning cups of coffee.

I snuggled down and rubbed the back of his neck. "Can you imagine, we have a son who is almost nineteen! Did you ever think we would have a child that old?"

"Sneaks up on you, doesn't it?" Bill said, arching his neck. "Ahh, that feels good."

"I haven't had a chance to tell you about the latest plans for Rusty's birthday party, have I?"

"No, what's going on now? I know you were concerned about having a party because all Rusty's friends live on the mainland."

"Well, we're going to have the party on the mainland."

"Really, how did that come about?"

"Mickey was talking to Mrs. Collins and she suggested we have the party at her house. I think that is very gracious of her. Is it okay with you?"

"Too right," he agreed. "We can take everything we need over on our boat. When is the party going to be?"

"Let's have it on a Sunday afternoon because a lot of the teens work on Saturdays."

"Sounds good to me. Let me know if I need to get any equipment for the entertainment."

After the girls helped make the invitations, I called the boys together for a conference on which games to play. We searched through our books on party games. "I like this one," Skippy laughed, pointing to a page he was reading.

I looked up from my book. "Tell me about it."

"It's a Spoon Contest. The players are in pairs. For each pair you tie two spoons six inches apart on a string. The race is to see which pair can finish a dish of ice cream first."

"I like the idea of the ice cream," Rusty said hesitantly, "but wouldn't it be kind of messy?"

"That's the fun of it," Skippy grinned, defending the game, "I think we'll get a lot of laughs."

"Mom, here's another good one," Mickey said holding out his book. "All we need are sheets of newspaper."

I read the directions. It was a Newspaper Race. Each contestant had two sheets of newspaper to step on. Getting to the finish line meant stepping on one and reaching behind to move the second one to the front. "That should stir up some excitement," I said. "Dealing with one age group at a time would work out well, too."

"I've got one," Rusty, the sportsman, offered. "It's called Lemonade Golf. With a long stick you roll a lemonade bottle across the floor to the finish line. All we need are some two-foot dowels and a lemonade bottle. The book says it's harder than it sounds. I know the boys can do it but I don't know about the girls."

It was one of our best parties. The kids, all different ages, played old fashioned "get right in there" party games. They were all simple but so much fun. Mr. Collins put a picnic table on the patio between the house and the garage. We piled it high with sandwiches, chips, nuts and other goodies. To quench dry throats we served gallons of lemonade, passion fruit punch and "cordial," (that's Australian for a fruit-flavored drink). Twenty hungry teens didn't leave anything to carry away. The huge homemade cake in the shape of a ship and blazing with nineteen candles was a great success.

Rusty and Mickey stayed over with friends. Skippy guided the boat home while Bill and I sat out on the deck and talked. "That was quite a party," Bill said. "Everyone had a wonderful time. I laughed so hard at the Lemonade Golf game my stomach hurt."

"It was funny, wasn't it? I thought it would never end. No one seemed to be able to control those jolly bottles."

Bill chuckled. "You should have seen the look on their faces when Rusty maneuvered his stick into the neck of his bottle and slid it across the finish line. It wasn't the way it was supposed to be played, but everybody was glad the game was over."

I smiled. "It amazes me that these kids who have just finished high school still enjoy party games and have no objection to the younger ones joining in. Very different from when we left the States six years ago. Teens were developing their own culture and separating themselves from the rest of the family."

"You're right," Bill said thoughtfully, "I just can't visualize this type of a party in the States. Life was already getting wild when we left. I can only imagine what it's like now. We're fortunate to be able to raise our children the old fashioned way."

"Yes, we are." I lifted a sleepy Topper onto my lap. "It's a shame that the island is going in the same direction."

Bill shook his head. "I understand that illegal beer is available at every function now."

"I've heard that, too. There seems to be a growing hostility between Russell and the other islands. And a deep rift on Russell itself. I'm thankful that we're not aware of all the shenanigans going on."

"Fair dinkum," Bill agreed, "I'm just waiting for someone to come along and offer us a princely price for our farm."

I laughed at his joke. "Hopefully it will get better with the new teacher," I soothed. "It seems that someone new is always coming when somebody else is leaving. Speaking of leaving, I wonder when Rusty will get a call from the shipping company."

"It could be any day now," Bill sighed as a tired Jackie climbed onto his lap. "It's going to be hard to see him go."

It was only two weeks later when the freight company rang us. They had an opening available on a ship going to the States. It would be a month en route and dock at Long Beach, California. My heart skipped a beat as I hung up the phone. I thought I was prepared to say goodbye to my oldest son but I wasn't. Where did the time go? Just yesterday, he was a freckle-faced boy slipping into, and out of,

A Son Is Grown

one adventure after another. America was so far away. When would we see him again?

"This will never do," I said, shaking myself, "you need to be happy for Rusty." I went to find Bill for comfort and reassurance.

Suddenly, there was so much to do. Apply for a passport. Get clothes ready. Bring down suitcases from the attic. Check and double check. I had no time to fret as we worked through the list. Much too quickly, it was time for Rusty to report to the ship. I went through the list one more time.

"Have you got everything?"

"Yes, ma'am."

"Do you have enough money?"

"Yes, ma'am."

"Will you write as soon as you can?"

"Yes, ma'am."

There was nothing more a mother could say. My boy had grown up.

The whole family went over to Brisbane to see him off. After goodbyes all around, we watched him climb the gangway to the ship. On the deck, he turned and waved goodbye before he was ushered below. I stood there, my eyes riveted to the empty space where Rusty had been standing. It was over so quickly.

Like all parents we were thrilled at having raised a child, but why does it hurt so much when they have to leave? Would he be all right? Had we taught him what he needed to know? I swallowed hard. Blinking back tears, I looked at Bill. "It's time to go," he said quietly.

We were a solemn group that pulled into the driveway at Fiddler's Green. I began to sing softly. We had passed another crisis. It was time to calm the waters. Bill looked at me and smiled. Our drooping spirits began to revive.

Life must go on.

Chapter Eighteen

A New Era

"Here's an airmail letter from Aunt Jac!" Mickey called, bounding up the stairs from collecting the mail at the post office.

"What does she say?" Bill asked, as I scanned the letter.

"She says her passport is in order and that she sails in July. Thank goodness for that. But, now she's wondering if her diet will be too difficult for us to cope with."

"What does she mean by that?" Bill asked, puzzled.

"She mentioned eggs, bread, raisins, Ritz Crackers and evaporated milk."

"Well," Mickey declared, "we have plenty of fresh eggs, that's for sure."

"Too right," Bill agreed, "but Australian raisins are a bit different. The evaporated milk and Ritz Crackers are the same, though."

I laughed. "Aunt Jac may be surprised to learn that in one month, our family consumes twenty pounds of brown rice, twelve pounds of wheat germ, forty loaves of whole wheat bread, ten pounds of unprocessed cheese and a twenty-eight-gallon tin of full-cream powdered milk. Plus bushels of fresh fruits and vegetables."

"That should satisfy her taste for natural foods," Bill said. "The only canned goods we use are dog food for Benji, tomato soup for sauces, baked beans for emergencies and tuna fish on Fridays."

"You forgot the thirty-six pounds of first-break cereal," Mickey reminded us. "It's going to taste different from the rolled oats she's using. And Australian sauces have a strong curry flavor."

"Gosh, yes. I remember how difficult it was for me to get used to the catsup. I think I'll write a note of encouragement while everyone is doing their chores."

Dear Aunt Jac,

You're getting on beautifully! We were a bit worried about your passport, since you didn't have a birth certificate on record. Bill is sending you all the information you need for your visas and is taking care of your entry nomination papers. He has just renewed his own passport. I'm sending you a copy of his picture. How we have aged in the past few years! And yet, I still meet people who say, "You have seven children!!"

The kids love the idea of being able to choose a grandmother. They liked the picture you sent. A hearty "she'll do" was their unanimous approval.

A New Era

Everyone is excited that you are coming. It's been such a long wait. I'm glad you decided to sail from Florida instead of going to England first. With the Suez Canal blocked because of the Arab-Israeli conflict, the trip from England around the cape would have taken six weeks.

You'll be docking in Sydney. That's about 600 miles from here. To come by car would take from twelve to fifteen hours. The train is almost as long, but you can sleep quite comfortably for most of the journey. We have a friend who visits the island once a year and finds it much easier to come by sleeper. In any case, Bill will meet you in Sydney and travel with you. When you get to Queensland, it will be an hour's drive from Brisbane to Redland Bay and one more hour by boat to Russell Island.

By the time you arrive at Fiddler's Green, we'll have a brand new ground level room for you. Since you've always been accustomed to a great deal of quiet and privacy, we'll try to make you as self-contained as possible. Then you can mingle when you please and retire when a big family overwhelms you.

Bill is making a little kitchen area for you to cook a bit of soup or brew a cup of tea. We have an extra refrigerator just outside your door. You'll find our kitchen empty and available most of the time—except during peak hours and then it's worth anyone's life to enter with all the activity that goes on there.

We do have a kitchen garden but so far parsley is my only herb. Perhaps you can help me with other herbs when you get settled. The boys have prepared an area just outside your row of windows for your own small garden.

I'm really sorry you missed Rusty. He left in June and is working his way back to the States on a freighter. He plans to go to college in Washington State this fall. Everyone else is doing well. Our best wishes for a wonderful trip.

Love and Blessings

The days passed rapidly. With so many preparations for Aunt Jac's arrival, there was little time to worry about Rusty. But he was always on my mind.

Finally, the outside of Aunt Jac's room was finished. The hard part was next. Bill removed the large wooden piers that supported the house in that area and replaced them with much smaller metal pipes. He installed windows and did the finishing work on the walls and closet.

We were busy mixing paint when Mickey showed up with the mail. "We have a telegram!" he called. Everyone stopped what they were doing and converged in the dining room. We watched anxiously as Mickey unloaded the mail from the tucker bag.

"A telegram!" I said, grabbing it out of his hand. "Who would send us a telegram?"

"Rusty?" Tia guessed.

I ripped it open and melted with relief. "It's from the Fergusons in Yakima. They say not to worry, Rusty arrived in Pomona alive and well. "Pomona?" my brow wrinkled, "what's he doing in Pomona?"

"Don't you remember?" Bill said, "he was planning to visit the Semenyeis before he went on to Washington."

"Oh yes!" I sighed. "With all the rush I forgot. Gosh, it seems like only yesterday that the Semenyeis came to the ship to say goodbye when we left for Australia. Well, anyway, thank God he arrived safely."

"How about celebrating with some cookies and milk?" Skippy suggested.

"Jolly good," I turned to Pam and Jackie. "Come help me fix the snack and then we'll all go back to work." Smiling at my twelve-year-old decorator apprentice, I told everyone, "Tia and I are ready to plan the interior of Aunt Jac's room."

"What are you using for furniture?" Mickey wanted to know.

"We have Rusty's single bed and bureau, my padded rocker, two kitchen chairs and a small table."

"Mom and I are going to Brisbane to pick out material for curtains and the spread," Tia said proudly.

By the end of the month, everything was ready. Pictures were hung on the walls. The rocking chair had taken over a cozy corner and the table and chairs sat invitingly in front of the windows. "It looks like something out of a *Good Housekeeping* magazine," Bill said, giving us his seal of approval.

"Aunt Jac used a lot of green in her house in Maine, so I think she'll be happy with the colors we chose." I smoothed the deep green and gold bedspread and straightened the gold accent pillow. I looked at Bill. "When will you be leaving for Sydney?"

"I'll go early on Thursday to catch the train from Brisbane. I want to be there on the dock when the ship comes in. Flying would have been quicker for Aunt Jac but much more strenuous. Fortunately, she loves sailing and really wanted to cross the ocean. Quite a feat for someone who's eighty-three years old."

The day before Bill left we got a letter from Rusty. He had spent two weeks visiting the Semenyeis. He wrote:

> *They rented a boat in Baja, Mexico. We had a great time spear fishing out in the gulf. I caught one of the biggest fishes I have ever hooked! It was a tuna—not a bluefin, but big enough to require two of us to get it into the boat. Tunas make for some good eating. We had a great feast!*
>
> *The Fergusons met me at the bus depot when I got to Washington. It's beautiful country up here. I already have a job at the Delmonte processing plant. All I do is sort lima beans but I'll be able to save money for college this fall.*
>
> *Love*
> *Your son, Rusty*

"That's our boy," Bill said proudly. "I'm so glad that letter came before I left."

The next morning he was on his way to Sydney. I spent the day polishing the house and planning Aunt Jac's welcome dinner. Wanting to make something Australian that a New Englander would like, I settled for "pumped" lamb. That's lamb that has been pumped with salt to make it taste like ham—and it does!

"Tomorrow is Saturday—no school," I told the girls.

"Oh, goody, can we make a cake?" Jackie begged.

"Yes, you may, and I'll let you decorate the table, too."

A New Era

With all the excitement it was hard to settle everyone at bedtime. I read an extra chapter of *The Famous Five* before they mellowed. It had been such a long day.

Early the next morning, two giggling girls crept into my room. "Isn't it a bit early to get up?" I murmured, hoping they would go away.

"No! Aunt Jac comes today and we have a lot to do," Jackie exclaimed.

"What's the weather like?" I stalled with my eyes still closed.

"It's sunny, Mom," Tia said, joining the other two with Topper bounding in behind her.

"Mommy, it's light," Topper announced. "Daddy's coming home. Can we go down to the boat to meet him?" At five years old, Topper was always ready to go.

Putting her arm around him, big sister Pam explained gently, "Topper, she won't be here until this afternoon."

Mickey stuck his head around the door. "Mom, do you want me to start breakfast? Skippy's out taking care of the chickens."

Defeated, I opened my eyes. "That would be wonderful Mickey. Tia, help Topper make his bed and put some clothes out for him to wear. Jackie, you and Pam make your beds and help Mickey if he needs you."

With the room cleared, I took a few minutes to stretch before crawling out of bed. "Well," I mused, "the big day we've been waiting for has arrived—at full speed."

The day continued to race along, leaving no time for anyone to ask, "When will they be here?" Suddenly it was boat time. The young ones pleaded, "Mom, can we go to the jetty with Mickey?"

"With all the luggage, there won't be room for you to ride back. But, if you want to, you can go down, say hello to Aunt Jac and walk home."

"Jolly good!" they shouted, running for the car.

"I'll stay here with you, Mom," Tia said unexpectedly.

We waved goodbye and they were off. We busied ourselves with last-minute preparations until we heard a familiar motor. "They're here!" Tia said, running to the stairs.

We reached the car as Bill was helping Aunt Jac out. She was just as I remembered, spry and petite. In a flurry of talk, we learned that she and Bill had visited the shops in Sidney while they were waiting for the train. Yes, they had been able to sleep well on the train. Yes, she had enjoyed the ocean voyage.

"No, I didn't get seasick," she assured us before we had a chance to ask.

Tia nudged me. "Can I show Aunt Jac her room?" she wanted to know. Ah, I thought, that's why she didn't go to the jetty.

"Certainly," I told her.

Tia led Aunt Jac to her new room. Bill and I stood quietly, waiting for her response. When we heard the "aah's" and "ooh's" coming from the room, I looked at Bill and smiled. "She's pleased," I said. "We have begun a new era in the Moore family."

That turned out to be an understatement. Each evening, Aunt Jac dominated the dinner conversation. At first, she entertained us with stories of Maine and adventures on her trip. As the days went by, she turned to the classics and expounded on the philosophies of men. She had grown up with the rule that *children should be seen but not heard*.

The situation became awkward. Our evening meal had always been an important time of family communication. With the children away all day, we needed this time to keep up with their lives.

Out in the gazebo with our morning cup of coffee, I asked Bill what I should do about it. "I'm torn between nurturing our children and hurting Aunt Jac's feelings."

"I don't know what you can do," he said, "but something needs to be done."

"The Swimming Pool"

Chapter Nineteen

God Still Does Miracles

Flushed with 1967's success, we made plans for an even bigger crop in 1968. We borrowed money from the bank for more fertilizer than ever before. We spent days tossing it around by the bucketful and waited for the rain so we could plant. History has since recorded that Queensland's most severe drought in eighty years reached its peak in the spring of 1968. Draining the meager water supply from our well, we planted at the crawling rate of five rows a day. The crop ran from disappointing to disastrous.

By mid-1969, we had no money and almost no food. It was one of the lowest points of our farming career. In order for me to keep a doctor appointment in Brisbane, we hunted through the house for enough coins to pay for my boat and bus fares. "If it wasn't such a necessary trip, I'd stay home," I told Bill.

"No," he said, "don't worry, everything will be all right."

After a long day in town, I sat on the deck of the ferry watching the off-shore breeze ruffling the water. The doctor's verdict had been, "It's something we need to keep an eye on." With a heavy heart I wondered what was going to happen next. We really need a miracle, I prayed as the boat carried me homeward.

Mickey met me at the jetty with a big grin. "Dad's got a surprise," he said.

"Fair dinkum?" I brightened, "what is it?"

"You'll have to wait," was all he would say.

Climbing the stairs, I was met with the wonderful aroma of meat sizzling in the pan. Meat? Where did that come from? I wondered. In the kitchen Bill was all smiles. "I want to show you something," he told me. He nodded at Mickey to take over the kitchen. We went downstairs where he pointed to a couple of potato sacks full of vegetables. "There's more stuff upstairs in the kitchen," he with a grin.

"Where did you get these?" I asked, struggling to believe my eyes.

"Remember Ron and Jack telling us about the land development company down at the other end of the island?"

"Yes."

"Well I went down there today to see if they needed a construction driver. It just so happened that the four-man crew they had brought over from the mainland didn't want to stay. So they hired me."

I sat down on the steps, stunned. "Amazing," I murmured.

"It gets better," Bill laughed. "As I was leaving, they asked me if I could use the food they had brought over to feed the men. I said sure. 'Please take as much as you can,' they said. So I did. This is some of it and there's more upstairs in the cupboard. "

I wasn't sure whether to laugh or cry. "Coming home on the boat," I told Bill, "I was asking God for a miracle and here it is." I was awed. "It's more than I could ever have imagined, and just when we needed it the most." Bill put his arm around my shoulder and together we went up the stairs to a feast.

He began working for Nichol's Development Company as a grader operator six days a week. He was making half the money Rusty earned sorting lima beans in Seattle. But this was Australia and we had money coming in.

Bill was enjoying his break from a farmer's never-ending battle with insects, elements, hours that slip by and work that never ends. I was enjoying the steady paycheck, money that came in on a regular basis without worrying about planting, irrigating or harvesting.

Even without farm work, there was still plenty to do. I laid block for retaining walls on each side of the pool area. I supervised the boy's farm chores. I taught myself to play the piano. I helped Aunt Jac adjust to island living. She was delighted with her room but spent most of her day up and down the stairs.

"It's a little frustrating," I told Bill, during our walk-talk time. "I have to stop what I'm doing to solve her problems. They're just little things, like what color thread she should use."

"She's bored," Bill diagnosed. "We need to get her involved with some of the ladies her age."

"Why didn't I think of that! It's a great idea. She always took long walks back home but she hasn't done that here. Tomorrow, Topper and I will take her down to meet Miss Watts."

We did. They immediately struck up a friendship, often going "walkabout" (Aussie word for wandering). Miss Watts was an authority on all plants and growing things. Aunt Jac was delighted with her new knowledge.

She told me about her latest walkabout. "We went out to Canaipa Road. On the way, a cobber stopped his lorry to say g'day," she said. "Nelly (she was referring to Miss Watts) told me the bloke was a good friend of yours. We said ta' for the offer of a ride, but we were going to boil the billy. We'll be stopping for a cuppa and bickies, I told him."

I was impressed with the number of Australian words Aunt Jac had picked up in such a short time. She was much more content and often went to the store by herself. She bought cookies and invited her friends in for afternoon tea. Soon everyone on the island knew Aunt Jac. She listened to the downtrodden and served tea to the sick. She put lovely hand-sewn touches on things I made on the machine. She visited around the island and left her younger friends exhausted. Life was good.

In September, Rusty wrote that he was deep into the routine of Yakima Community College. *"College is different from high school,"* he wrote. *"In Biology the teacher doesn't lecture, he assigns work and gives a test on Friday. The lab teacher vaporizes shortly after class starts."*

"College hasn't changed has it?" I grinned.

The letter continued… *"I went hunting with Mr. Ferguson and shot my first deer. I had the butcher cut it into steaks, with some parts ground for mince to put in the freezer. I'm all set for weeks of good eating."*

"Listen to what he eats," I said with pride. *"My daily menu is, for breakfast: bacon, eggs, cereal or pancakes. At lunch I have meat and tomato, or peanut paste and jam sandwiches. Dinner is usually ground mince, salad, vegetables and fruit. I drink milk or orange juice."*

Bill chuckled. "Years of nutritional training and time in the kitchen, is paying off. At least we know he is able to feed himself well."

Later, when Rusty learned that his dad was working off the farm, he wrote again. *"If the farm is doing badly and you need help, I could get a job to earn money to send home," he offered.* My heart swelled with pride. We had "raised a fine boy," as my grandmother would say.

"You had better write back right away," Bill was concerned. "We wouldn't want him to do anything foolish like leave college to go to work. I'm pleased that he offered but that would never do."

Soon after that, we had another big event. I couldn't wait for Bill to come home from work. I had found an advertisement for above-ground pools, something new in Australia. I heard his truck coming and was waiting for him in the yard. "Hon, guess what!"

"The house burned down," he guessed. It would have to be pretty serious for his wife to meet him in the driveway.

"No, silly. It's the swimming pool.

"We don't have a swimming pool." He headed for the stairs.

"But we can," I insisted, thrusting the advertisement at him.

He paused, scanning it. "Oh," he said. "Let's go upstairs and talk about it."

He read the ad while I fixed his tea. "This may be a good idea," he said when he finished. "When we had the money to build the pool, we were too busy with crops to do anything about it. When we had the time to build the pool we didn't have the money."

"Too right," I agreed. "But this seems to be the answer. It's not as expensive an in-ground pool and we can do it all ourselves. No cement to pour, no cement to cure and we already have the area for it."

"Now I can see why you were so excited," he grinned. "The kids will love it. They've been waiting for so long. I'll see about it tomorrow."

Bill ordered the round, twenty-four-foot across, above-ground plastic pool. When the huge boxes arrived, the barge truck drove them up to the house. They were able to unload them right next to the pool area. Topper was the only child at home. He was sure we would all be swimming by afternoon.

Bill found the directions and began to read. "The pool must be placed on a bed of sand. The area must be level and smooth. Remove all sharp items such as rocks..." He looked up. "This is going to take a while," he announced.

He was right. He and the boys spent weekends hauling countless trailer loads of sand from the other end of the island. They smoothed it out and raked it over and over to remove any rocks or bits of shells. Finally, they set up the rim and put the liner into place.

When they finished, Topper came running up to the house. "Come, come look, Mom! All we need is water."

I went down to admire the pool. It was beautiful and almost ready. Just in time for summer, too. Bill was busy hooking up the pump and the filter system. "Where are the boys?" I asked.

"They went up to the well to run the irrigation pipe down here. As soon as I finish this, we can start filling the pool."

"How long do you think it will take? I know the well is real low because of the drought."

He scanned the pool area. "Twenty-four feet across and four feet deep... about a week," he guessed. "At least there will be enough water to play in by then."

He was right, as always. Each day they pumped as much water as they could. By the end of the week the filter system was able to operate. Each day when the children came home from school, their first question was, "Is it ready yet?"

On Saturday at dinner, Dad announced, "We're having a party tomorrow." They all looked at each other, wondering whose birthday it was. Finally, Pam asked, "What kind of party?"

"I know," Topper shouted, "a swimming party!"

Everyone began to talk at once. Is the pool ready? Is it full enough? Can we really swim in it? "Yes, yes, yes," Dad answered. "Tomorrow, we'll move the picnic table down in the shade between the tennis court and the pool. We'll have our picnic celebration there." We hadn't seen so much excitement since Aunt Jac came.

Bill brought a comfortable lawn chair down for her. The children urged her to join them in the pool, but she only smiled and said, "I'll just sit here in the shade and watch you swim." The children jumped, splashed, played games and shouted for us to watch their latest accomplishment. Topper played around the edge of the pool; he wasn't quite ready to take the plunge.

A private swimming pool was a novel idea on Russell Island. All summer long, we had the children's mainland friends and their parents over to Fiddler's Green for barbecues and swims. Our 1930s-style farm had blossomed into a six-bedroom home with electricity and proper plumbing. In the front was a circular drive, in the back a tennis court, picnic area and beautifully landscaped swimming pool. It was, indeed, a miracle.

Chapter Twenty

Growing Pains

In the normal progression of things, Mickey passed his tenth grade Junior Public Exam and started his sub-senior school year. Mickey was a nice kid. In his spare time he was my landscape gardener and did a beautiful job. But because he was seventeen we sometimes clashed. Such as on the day his shirt wasn't ironed to his liking.

"You've ironed my collar flat again!" he said, scrutinizing his uniform shirt.

"How was I supposed to iron it?"

"Nobody wears a flat collar any more," he growled, buttoning the offending shirt. "Goodbye, God bless you," he muttered as he stomped through the kitchen and down the stairs. I suspected he didn't intend God to do any such thing. Unless it was to bless me with a bit more knowledge of how to iron a shirt collar.

"You've made my lunch all wrong," nine-year-old Pam scolded from the kitchen.

"What do you mean?" I asked, standing with the hair brush poised in mid-air—seven-year-old Jackie had just dashed off to hunt for her ponytail elastics.

"They're cut square!" Pam grumbled.

I called to Jackie, "Hurry up with the elastics or you'll be late for the boat." After the last minute bustle of tying up ponytails, gathering back packs and lunch boxes, they were off calling, "God bless you" as they hurried down the steps.

Alone, I sank into the nearest chair with a depressed sigh. We were just getting into a new school year. Suddenly, they were all trying to adapt to the expectations of their schoolmates.

Mickey was the most difficult to cope with. He had changed from peanut paste to Vegemite, Australian for a thick, brown sandwich spread made from brewer's yeast. Vegemite, with its strong, tart flavor, described his temperament. He had become sullen, silent and uncooperative, always finding fault with something.

Life hadn't been this grim since Rusty had turned seventeen. The quick flashes of temper, the sulks and later... "I'm sorry," Rusty would say, "I just don't know what got into me." And then, a discussion of the painful process of becoming an adult, until, slowly, the bridge was built.

But not Mickey. He'd be the last person to admit having faults.

"Well," I sighed, "now that I know the situation, it's time to do something about it." Vegemite for lunch instead of peanut paste. Extra elastics on hand for Jackie.

Cut Pam's sandwiches diagonally. Square sandwiches and flat collars are out.

The next morning the others had left, before Mickey made his discovery. "There's no clean shirt here!"

"No dear, but there is one on the ironing board."

"It isn't done and I'm late!"

"Well, you shouted yesterday because it wasn't ironed right, so I thought I'd let you do it yourself today. The book that tells how to use the iron is on top of the bookcase. I'm going down to start the laundry." Anticipating an explosion, I hastily closed the door and headed downstairs. If I could just wash out his mouth with soap! Turn him over my knee! Stand him in a corner! Shout at him!

Thoughts of the past few weeks of insults, snubs and complaints carried me to the tool shed and on to the garden with a trowel in my hand. The laundry just wasn't far enough away. "Oh!" I muttered as I jabbed at the earth, "how can someone who shaves every day be such a brat!"

I reflected wistfully on the times Rusty had come into the kitchen after school. "Do you want any help?" he would offer. As he peeled potatoes, he would ask for advice on girls and we would talk. But Mickey was Mickey. Yanking at the weeds, I comforted myself: "In time they all grow up."

The next day an ungrateful twelve-year-old was giving me angry instructions on how to sew on her uniform button. "Mothers get very tired of doing things for children who always find fault but never say thank you. Here, you can sew on your own button." I handed her the dress and went back to the kitchen.

You're not alone Mickey, everyone has to learn. Even if he didn't offer to help in the kitchen after school, Mickey did many other things to help. I recalled the note I had sent to school just a week ago:

Dear Mr. Clooney,

Michael tells me you do not approve of his leaving the school grounds at lunch time. I'm sure it is only because you do not realize our situation. Except for a few items of food sold on the island, our only recourse to shopping is spending an entire day going to Brisbane and back. Fares total $1.90, not counting trams or lunch. One can only buy as much as one can carry. With a large family such as ours, one cannot afford to go to town often. Having a child in high school who is able to do errands during lunch hour is a blessing. In closing, let me assure you that Michael is not being sent into Cleveland for trivial reasons.

That night during our evening walk, I poured out my frustration to Bill. "I know," he sympathized. "I remember Rusty at that age. But he did grow up and look how well he turned out."

"Yes, but can I survive another seventeen year old?" I fumed.

"You can do it," he comforted me. "Think of Skippy, he's almost as tall as I am and beginning to come out of his shell. And he's collected an impressive number of sports awards this year. At least he's working hard at something."

"You're right. We do have to count our blessings. Tia did a bang-up job with dinner last night. She did all the cooking, from soup to dessert. Serving it with a lace tablecloth and candles was her idea. Perhaps her twelfth year will be a stormy one, but we've just shared a wonderful eleventh year." I heaved a sigh. "It's a good thing they aren't all going through the same stage at the same time."

Bill stopped to pick a couple of roadside ferns to swish away the mosquitoes that were buzzing around our faces. "Has it helped to have Pam and Jackie in separate rooms?"

"Yes, Pam loves the blackboard you made for her. She uses it to write lessons for her pretend class. The other day I heard her banging away and went to investigate. She was pounding on the chair with her wooden ruler looking angry and frustrated. I asked, 'What's the matter Pam?'

'I'm trying to make my class pay attention!' she said.

'Do you have to bang like that?'

'That's how my teacher does it,' she explained."

We walked quietly for a while, both wishing that we didn't have to send the younger children over to the mainland school.

Bill broke the silence. "Does Pam still depend on Jackie for small services such as tying her shoes?"

I couldn't help laughing. "At nine, you would think she could tie her own shoes. But if Jackie doesn't mind doing it, why should she bother? They are so different but they get along so well."

Bill chuckled. "Jackie is a little sausage. She still loves to be cuddled."

"Too right," I agreed. "Capable, smart as a tack and she still sucks her thumb. I wonder how much longer that will last. Hey! Turn on your torch. I think there's a snake in the road."

"It is. Look at it go! I'd better keep the light on for a while. Where there's one snake there is usually another."

"Ugh! Was it the deadly kind?"

"I couldn't tell. It's too dark to see the markings. Anyway, it's time to start back home. Tell me about Topper," he said, trying to take my mind off the snake.

"Today, I found him in the kitchen with a two-pound jar of peanut paste. He had screwed the end of a string under the cap and looped the other end over the cupboard door knob. He was using the knob as a pulley to hoist the jar up. Visualizing peanut butter splattered all over the place, I quickly slid my hand under the jar, in case the string broke. I asked him what he was doing. He told me he was putting the peanut paste back up on the shelf."

Bill laughed. "That's Topper, always figuring out the best way to get a job done. Do you think he'll drive his teacher nuts next year?"

"I don't know about that, but he's finally joined the others in the pool instead of playing around outside of it. They spend hours jumping in and climbing out. In the water they're like a school of fish."

"Wonderful," Bill said. "We were lucky to find an above-ground pool in Australia. If we had had to wait until I could build one, we would still be waiting."

"Mickey, bless his heart, has already planned the landscaping. He's going to plant flowering ground cover on the slopes going down to the pool area and flowering plants that will hang over the edge of the retaining walls. It will look very nice when he finishes."

"We're home," Bill said heading across the lawn, "let's have a cuppa before we go to bed. Tomorrow is another day. Who knows what that will bring."

"That's right," I agreed, "it jolly well may be the day Mickey turns into a happy adult!"

Chapter Twenty-One

Surprises

Bill's construction job came to an end when Nichols Company finished their contract. He replaced it with a job harvesting tomatoes on a farm at Redland Bay. When that finished, he got a job driving a taxi in Brisbane. "It won't be for long," he promised. "The drought is bound to break soon."

At least he was at home on the weekends to spend some time with the children. We planted crops as the water situation allowed. During the week the boys and I were able to take care of the few acres we had growing. It was a whole new kind of life, but it was never dull.

Christmas that year brought another vintage car into the family. The ancient Oldsmobile had been parked in the "hold-for-spare-parts area." It had always been a difficult car to start but, finally, it wouldn't start at all. Bill bought a 1950 Holden sedan on the mainland. He brought it over to the island, hoping to make another truck like the Ladybug.

As soon as the Holden arrived, Mickey, an avid car enthusiast, rushed out to give it a good going over. He was back in no time with a report. Starting in the middle of the subject, he informed his dad, "You can't make a truck out of it."

"Why not? It shouldn't be any problem. We did it before."

"It doesn't have a frame." Mickey said.

"What do you mean?" Bill asked. "All cars have a frame."

"I know, but Mr. Wilson came by while I was looking at the car. He said the American GMC cars are made differently than the English Vanguard. This one won't work."

"That's crook," Bill said. "Well…at least we'll be able to ride to the jetty without getting wet or covered with dust."

Right from the start, the "Beaut Bomb," as he dubbed it, was Mickey's baby, a six-cylinder car with a six-volt battery, it was very temperamental and stopped often. Mickey told me he had the right "touch" to get it started again.

Since Bill was working on the mainland, it was Mickey's job to drive everyone to the jetty for the school boat. He parked the car at the jetty compound to be ready for the return trip after school. The Beaut Bomb saved the girls from long, daily walks with heavy backpacks.

Skippy used the car too, but he was more… thump, bang and no go. Often he would send an S.O.S home. "I'm stalled down at Canaipa. Come on down with the tractor and get me started." After the seven-mile drive on the tractor to rescue Skippy, Mickey would gently start the Beaut Bomb and ride comfortably back to the farm leaving Skippy to bump home on the tractor.

Surprises

One day, when Mickey was away, Skippy drove the Beaut Bomb to the other end of the island with Topper. I was working in the flower garden out front by our new circular driveway. We had decided to spruce up the center of the drive by adding a border of flowers. I looked up as Skippy came running into the yard. "Can I take the tractor?" he asked hurriedly. "The car won't start."

"Yes, but where's Topper?"

"He's watching the car. We'll be back pretty soon." He climbed up on the tractor and started off before I could ask any more questions. In a hurry to get back to Topper, I supposed.

As I watched him disappear down the road, I wondered, *how is he going to get both the tractor and the car back to Fiddler's Green? I should have gone with him. Well, it's too late now.*

Concentrating on weeding and planting, I lost track of time—until I heard the motor. Even at a distance, I knew it was our tractor coming up the road. "He's going much too fast," I fumed. "Will he ever learn?"

The tractor zoomed into the yard and came to a halt. I looked up, ready to give Skippy a good scolding for reckless driving, but I couldn't see him. He wasn't there. "Well. I know that thing didn't drive itself." I put down my trowel and stood up. Topper jumped down from the tractor. He was so little, I hadn't seen him until I stood up.

"Where's Skippy?" I knew he had to be there. But where?

"He's coming with the car," Topper said, importantly.

Suddenly, realizing what an incredibly dangerous thing had just taken place, I felt as though I was going into a state of shock. I muttered faintly, "Don't tell me… you drove that tractor… all the way from Canaipa?"

"Yes," he said proudly, "Skippy told me it would be all right."

"But you can't even reach the brakes." I wanted to scream, but I didn't.

"Skippy said to turn the key off when I wanted to stop. He told me to push that little lever down if I wanted to go slower. You know," he wiggled his finger up and down, "that thing by the steering wheel." He grinned, "I moved it up and went faster."

I sat down. There are times when there is nothing left to say. This was too much. I thought of that huge tractor. It had wheels almost five feet tall and wide enough to flatten anybody twice Topper's size.

Tractors are an important part of farm life. They are used for many things. But not this. It was not a vehicle for a five-year-old. My mind flashed back to Topper's "broom-broom." It was a toddler's three-wheeled kiddie cart. No pedals, just foot power. Bill had fixed a 12x9-inch zucchini packing case to the back end for a "truck" bed.

When he was two years old, Topper would push his broom-broom up to the field where we were working. He'd wait patiently for someone to "load" his truck with three or four potatoes. With a full load, he would happily scoot his truck all the way back to the house. Topper always acted out what he saw others doing. It didn't matter whether he was big enough or not. "God help us," I prayed.

I stood up. "Topper, come here." I put my hands on his shoulders and looked down into his eyes. "You did a good job driving that tractor home. But I don't want you ever to drive it again without asking me first. Do you understand?" He nodded. "I don't care what your brothers say; you remember what your mother said."

"Yes, ma'am," he said solemnly, looking up at me. Wearily, I took his hand. "Come on, let's go into the house."

Later, when I scolded Skippy, he defended himself. "It was all right, Mom. Topper drives the tractor in the fields."

I shook my head. "The road to Canaipa is not the fields. Five years old and he can swim, ride a bike and row a boat. Am I supposed to add 'drive a tractor' to his list of accomplishments? No," I answered my own question emphatically. With my I-really-mean-it voice, I told him never to do that again.

Although we seem to slide backwards at times, there is progress.... Our most outstanding achievement for the year was finishing the job of painting the house. Climbing into bed, I told Bill, "It's like getting a gold star on your good behavior chart."

"Fair dinkum," he said. "It took us four years, four months and three weeks from start to finish, inside and out! Our bedroom was supposed to be first but it ended up being last."

"It was worth it, Hon. I love the way the room looks, it's so... 'stateside.' I may regret having a white organdy bedspread living on a red soil island, but it makes the room beautiful. I'm glad you took that old carpet out. The polished wood floor and gold throw rugs are just right. The whole room feels different. It's bright and pretty."

"Straight from *Good Housekeeping*!" Tia called from her bedroom next door.

"Too right!" I called back, "the white sheers you chose for the windows look wonderful! You and I turned out to be very good decorators."

"Thanks. Good night, Mom, good night, Dad."

"Now go to sleep," I told her, "you have to get up for school tomorrow."

A few weeks later, a young man knocked on the door. Bill was working in town and the children were on their way to school. I was the only one at home. Who could be calling this time of day? I wondered. At the front door, too. He must have come over on the early boat. Perhaps another preacher.

When I opened the door, he introduced himself. "Good morning," he said, "I'm a real estate agent. Your husband sent me around to have a look at the place. He's put it on the market."

I was stunned. I didn't know what to say. Speechless, I stepped back and beckoned him in.

Order Form

Moore Family Odyssey *You've Got to Be Kidding!* Series

❑ Book One: *Move to Australia?*   ISBN 1-55306-438-0
❑ Book Two: *Me? An Australian Farmer?* ISBN 1-55306-637-5
❑ Book Three: *Sell Our Australian Farm?*   ISBN 1-55306-860-2

Please print:

Name: _____

Address: _____

City: _____   State/Prov: _____

Zip/Postal Code: _____ Telephone: _____

_____ copies @ $14.95 US/$22.00 CDN.: $_____

Shipping: ($1.50 first book – $1.00 each add. book) $_____

Total amount enclosed: $_____

Payable by Check or Postal Money Order

(Please make checks payable to Connie Moore.
Allow two to three weeks for delivery.)

Send to: *Connie Moore*
                     9701 E Hwy #25, Lot 176
                     Belleview, FL 34420
                     USA